The Official FA

ENGLAND ANNUAL 1990

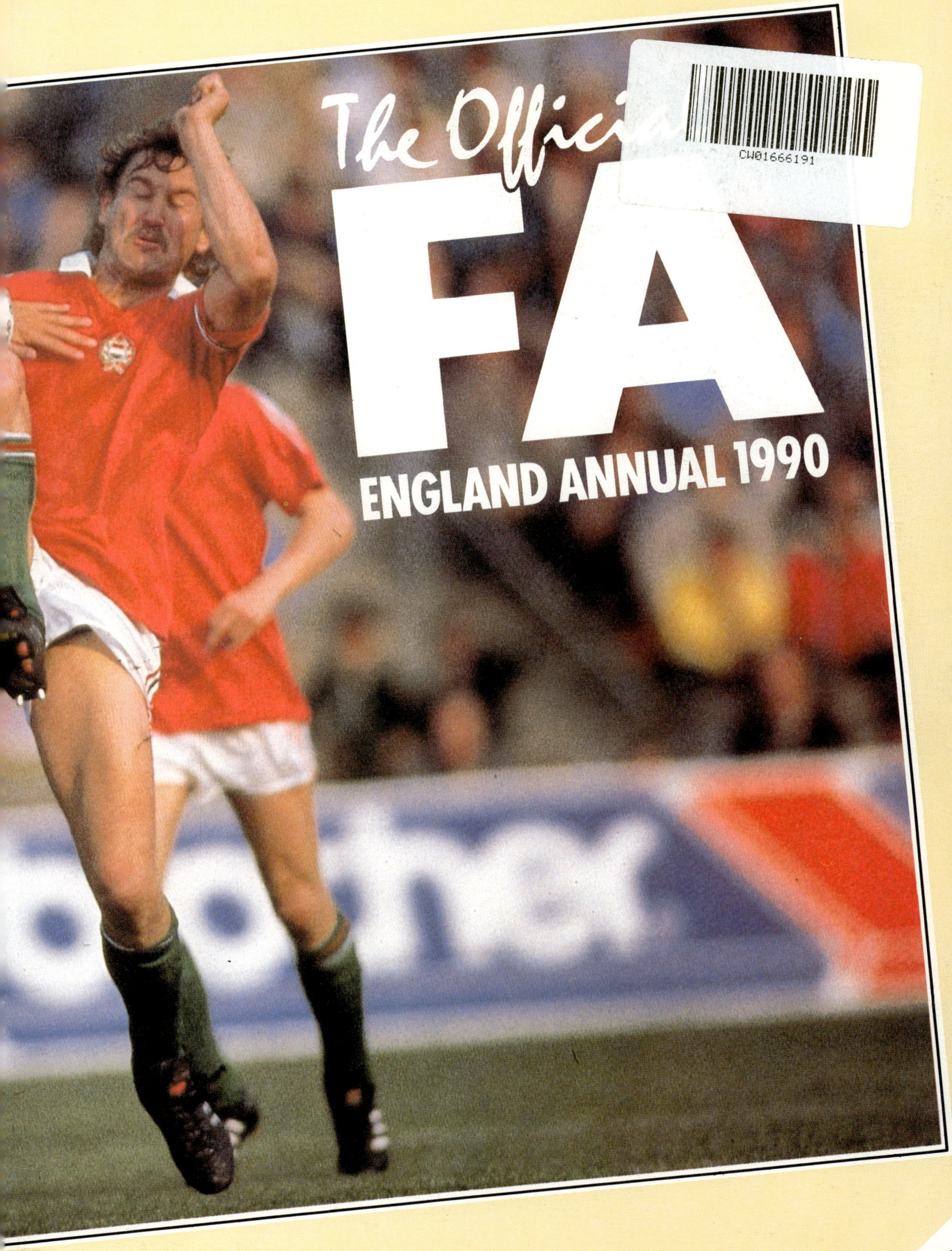

£3·99

Contents

Published in Great Britain by World International Publishing Limited,
An Egmont Company, Egmont House, P.O.Box 111, Great Ducie Street, Manchester M60 3BL.
Printed in Italy. ISBN 0 7235 6860 X

Acknowledgements
The colour photographs in this annual are by Bob Thomas Sports Photography with the following exceptions: Action Images Sports Picture Library (16, 17, 21); All-Sport Photographic Ltd (25); British Satellite Broadcasting (48, 49); Budget Rent A Car (53); Colorsport (24, top left); The Football Association (27, 42, 43); John Maiden (51); R A Simpson (41); Syndication International (1986) Ltd (24, bottom right); Wembley Stadium Ltd (26, 37).

The FA England Annual has been written by The Football Association unless indicated otherwise and with the exception of pages 24–25; 48–49; 53. Edited by John Malam and designed by Brian Folkard.

Cover photographs (top to bottom):
Nigel Clough; Paul Gascoigne; Gary Lineker (inset); Peter Beardsley; Bryan Robson; Chris Waddle.

THE FOOTBALL ASSOCIATION
LIMITED
Founded 1863

Patron: HER MAJESTY THE QUEEN
President: H.R.H. THE DUKE OF KENT
Chairman: F. A. MILLICHIP

Chief Executive:
R. H. G. KELLY FCIS

Phone: 01-402 7151/262 4542
Telex: 261110
Facsimile: 01-402 0486

16 LANCASTER GATE, LONDON W2 3LW

Dear England Supporter,

WELCOME TO THE VERY FIRST OFFICIAL FA ENGLAND ANNUAL

Ever since I can remember, I've been mad about soccer.

When I was younger, I spent all of my time reading or talking about soccer - when I wasn't out playing or training. This annual would have been right up my street in those days. Come to think of it, it is now! I'm sure you'll feel the same.

The Official FA England Annual is packed with great articles, pictures and a superb competition with great prizes to be won!

Read about what goes on behind the scenes when the England squad gets together. Learn how you can practise your skills and become a Soccer Star. Find out lots of things you never knew about the players in our international side, and much, much more.

Don't forget to enter for the top-prize England Who's Who Competition on page 58. Who knows, it might be you who meets the England players one day soon.

Good luck and good reading!

Bobby Robson

BOBBY ROBSON
England Team Manager

Registered Office: 16 Lancaster Gate, London W2 3LW
Incorporated in London Registration Number 77797

KICK-OFF FOR

the start of international football

◀ *The England team line-up that played against Germany in 1899*

An England team group from the 1950s with the players resplendent in their tasseled caps ▶

◀ *The 1959 England squad at Ninian Park, Cardiff. The match against Wales ended in a 1–1 draw and the England side included Bobby Charlton, Don Howe, Jimmy Greaves and Brian Clough*

ENGLAND

A famous programme from a famous match – the World Cup Final, 1966, when England beat West Germany 4–2 at Wembley

The first international football matches played anywhere in the world were those between England and Scotland in the 1870s. The series owed its beginning to the enterprise of C.W. Alcock, the first full-time Secretary of The Football Association. He wrote a letter to *The Sportsman* newspaper, announcing that a match between "the leading representatives of the Scotch and English sections" was to be played under the auspices of the FA and that players were being invited to submit their names for selection.

The first time that England played Scotland north of the border – at the ground of the West of Scotland Cricket Club at Partick, near Glasgow, on Saturday 30 November, 1872 – is now accepted as being the first official international match in history. The match ended in a goal-less draw and was watched by a crowd of 4,000.

Within ten years both Wales and Ireland had joined the football family, and the first Home International Championship series was held in 1884 with Scotland the first winners. But Britain was way ahead of the rest of the world in terms of international football. The first international match on the European continent was not played until 1902 (Austria *v* Hungary) and the first in South America not until 1905 (Argentina *v* Uruguay). The first official international match between any of the home countries and a foreign country was that between England and Austria, in Vienna in 1908.

England's first defeat abroad, with a team including professionals, was against Spain in Madrid in 1929 (4–3). The first home defeat, outside the Home Internationals, was not registered until Eire won 2–0 at Goodison Park in 1949, but the belief that England were the best in the world persisted until the 'Magical Magyars' of Hungary gave England a footballing lesson at Wembley in 1953, winning 6–3.

In 1950, the Home Internationals were made part of the qualifying competition for the World Cup tournament, and England, as winners, went to the finals in Brazil. It is now a matter of history that England's first participation in one of the most important international sporting competitions in the world turned out to be nothing short of a disaster. In their second group match in Belo Horizonte, England lost 1–0 to the rank outsiders – the United States. When the result was first seen in print, it was taken to be a mistake. Surely the correct score had been 10–1 to England!

As host country, England automatically qualified for the World Cup Finals in 1966. They went on to win the coveted Jules Rimet Trophy with some determined football and a well-organised defence which conceded just one goal in the five matches leading up to the final tie against West Germany – which England won 4–2. The victory gave such a boost to the English game that attendances at league matches went up by nearly three million over the next two years and the number of affiliated clubs in the country shot up by several thousand.

GETTING THE SQ

Saturday – 11 days to go

Bobby Robson, England Team Manager, goes to see a Barclays Football League match to check on the form of one or two players.

Monday – 9 days to go

He has decided who will be the twenty-two players to make up his international squad. He gives the names to Alan Odell, who runs The Football Association's international department. Alan puts letters in the post to all the clubs whose players have been picked telling them where and when they should report. At the same time, an Under-21 team has been chosen and letters are sent to their clubs.

Tuesday – 8 days to go

Bobby Robson holds a Press Conference at The Football Association's headquarters in Lancaster Gate, London, to tell all the newspapers which players have been picked and answer any questions the football journalists might have. David Bloomfield, the FA's Press Officer, gives all of the writers a list with the number of caps each player has got and the goals he has scored for England.

John Barnes leaves the team coach before a training session in Athens

Wednesday – 7 days to go

The first player pulls out of the squad, when Chris Waddle strains his groin in a cup replay. The manager doesn't feel the need to bring anyone else in.

Saturday – 4 days to go

A full Barclays League programme. The team loses Paul Davis, Tony Adams, Tony Dorigo and Ian Snodin injured. The players' clubs phone Alan Odell to let him know. He tells Bobby Robson, who decides to call in Gary Pallister. Alan Odell gets in touch with Bruce Rioch, the Middlesbrough manager, and asks him to let Pallister know. He reminds him that he must bring his boots and his passport! There are also two or three players injured in the Under-21 squad, so they have to be replaced, too.

Sunday – 3 days to go

John, the coach driver, comes to Lancaster Gate and picks up all of the equipment for the two teams, which has been packed by Martin Grogan in the FA's kit room. The team has to take not only shirts and shorts, studs, shin-pads and training-gear – all the things you would normally think of – but also medicines and bandages (in case of injury or illness), food, and presents for the teams England will be playing against. At 6.00 p.m. the players start reporting in to the Chiltern Hotel, Luton. They stay at Luton because the team usually flies by charter plane.

David Batty has been called into the Under-21s, but turns up without his passport – it's locked up in the safe at Leeds United! Brian Scott, the team's travel agent, says not to worry, we can get him onto the plane without one.

UAD TOGETHER

Fortunately, the team is going to Greece, which is in the Common Market, so it shouldn't be too much of a problem.

Above. Waving the flag at the match. Ken Bailey, a dedicated England fan, is a familiar character at international matches and at those of AFC Bournemouth, his local club

Monday – 2 days to go

At 8.30 a.m., the two teams drive to Luton Airport, where Brian Scott is waiting with boarding passes. The flight leaves on time and three hours later everybody is in Greece. Three coaches are waiting. One for the first team, one for the Press, and another for the Under-21s. The Under-21s have a long drive to Patras. The first team only have a twenty minute drive into Athens. Fred Street and Norman Medhurst, the physiotherapists, make sure all the equipment is in the kit room. John Crane, the doctor, checks that dinner has been properly arranged and Bobby Robson talks to Kostas, the man from the Greek Football Association, about training sessions.

Left. Fred Street and Norman Medhurst, the team's physiotherapists, in the dressing-room before the match

Tuesday – 1 day to go

The players train at the Olympic Stadium, in Athens. Afterwards, Bobby Robson has another Press Conference to tell the journalists who will be playing. Des Walker and Alan Smith, both of whom will be winning their first caps, come and talk to the Press. The Under-21s lose 1–0.

Wednesday – the day of the match

While the players rest, some of the officials go to see the Acropolis. They don't make it, because the bus gets stuck half-way down a one-way street. At 1.00 p.m., the team coach leaves for the ground with a police escort. Fred Street and Norman Medhurst are already at the ground and when the players arrive, all of their strip has been laid out ready for them. At 2.55 p.m. the Greek team runs out to a big cheer and the England team to a smaller one. There is another roar within a minute of the kick-off, when the Greeks score from a penalty, but by the end of the match England have won 2–1 with goals by John Barnes and Bryan Robson.

Bobby Robson and the players have to do interviews for the Press and TV, but by 5.45 p.m. everybody is on the coach and ready to go to the airport. At 8.15 p.m. the team is in the air and on the way back to England. By 10.30 p.m. the plane has landed at Luton, everyone is through customs and on their way home, looking forward to the next time they can wear the England strip.

Soccer Knowledge?

1
Which club play their home matches at Home Park?

2
Pele played for which Brazilian club?

3
Name the only non-English team to win the FA Cup.

4
Name the only club whose ground is in England but who play in the Scottish Football League.

5
Which was the first club to install an artificial playing surface?

6
Rodney Marsh, George Best, Bobby Moore and Bobby Robson all played for which club?

7
Is the Goldstone Ground in Brighton or Hove?

8
Who defeated Leeds United in the 1973 FA Cup Final to cause a major upset?

9
If the Owls were at home to Wolves, who would be playing?

10
Which club was the first to defeat Tottenham Hotspur in their eighth FA Cup Final appearance?

11
If the Hornets were at home to the Bees, who would be playing?

12
Who won the first League Championship to be played after World War II?

13
Who is the youngest player to have played in the World Cup Finals?

14
If the Hatters were entertaining the Cobblers, who would be playing?

15
Who is the youngest player to have played in an FA Cup Final?

16
Which club started the inflatable banana craze?

17
Bobby Charlton played for Manchester United. Who did his brother Jackie play for?

18
Which club plays at Nou Camp?

19
If the Canaries were playing the Eagles, which two teams would be playing?

20
Can you have a square football pitch?

21
How far is the penalty spot from the goal-line?

22
Which two clubs play at Selhurst Park?

23
Can a goal be scored directly from: a) a corner kick, b) a throw in?

24
Which is the oldest Football League Club?

25
Which country is staging the 1990 World Cup Finals?

Answers on page 61.

ENGLAND'S

It is the exploits of the England senior team which receive most publicity, and rightly so, but during any one season the FA actually organises up to fifty international matches at eight different levels. There are games at senior, 'B', Under-21, Under-18, Under-17, Under-16, Under-15 and semi-professional levels.

Dave Sexton proudly holds the European Under-21 Championship trophy after England's 3–0 aggregate victory against Spain in 1984

England 'B' team

'B' Internationals, of which a few had been played in the 1950s, were re-introduced into the football calendar by England manager Ron Greenwood in 1978. The idea was to bridge the gap between Under-21 and senior levels. Matches have been played infrequently since then, with Bobby Robson, Howard Wilkinson and Graham Taylor in charge of the team at various times. There hasn't been a home match since 1984, when New Zealand were beaten 2–0 at Nottingham Forest's ground. A three-match tour against Switzerland, Norway and Iceland was played in 1989.

England Under-21 team

The England Under-21 team has been the best in Europe over the last few seasons. It plays in the European Championship run by UEFA and has reached at least the semi-final stage in all six of the competitions held so far. With thirty countries entering each time, this is quite an achievement.

England, with Dave Sexton as manager, were winners in 1982 and 1984, beating West Germany and Spain in the respective finals. A large number of the Under-21 players progress to the senior team, and their experience of playing in tough, competitive international matches always stands them in good stead. These players include Bryan Robson, Terry Butcher, Glenn Hoddle and Mark Hateley. Strangely, the player with the most Under-21 caps, Gary Owen, of Manchester City and West Bromwich Albion, never made the senior team.

England Youth Team

The England Youth Team is generally made up of players who are under 18 years old at the start of the season. This team has played in the European Youth Championship, formerly the International Youth Tournament, since 1948 with a fair amount of success. England won the Tournament in 1948, 1963, 1964, 1971, 1972, 1973, 1975 and 1980 (eight times all told), under various managers who have included Pat Welton, Ken Burton and John Cartwright.

Most players in the England Youth Team go on to play as professionals in the football league and a few make it to more senior England teams. The 'Class of 1980', which

TEAMS

defeated Poland 2–1 in the European Youth Final in Leipzig, lined up like this: Kendall, Banfield, Barnes, Peake, Caton, Mackenzie, Connor, Hateley, Mabbutt, Allen and Pates. There are some well-known names there.

Steve Bull

England Under-15 and Under-16 teams
The internationals organised by the FA at Under-15 and Under-16 levels feature players in the England team who are currently pupils at the GM Vauxhall FA National School at Lilleshall, Shropshire, where the cream of our young footballing talent spend two years receiving the best coaching available.

England semi-professional team
The top players from the GM Vauxhall Conference, and other leagues like the Vauxhall–Opel and the Northern Premier, have a chance of being selected for the England semi-professional team. This team has competed in the Four Nations Tournament, along with Scotland, Holland and Italy, and usually has a warm-up match before that against Wales. The team managers have been Keith Wright, Kevin Verity and Tony Jennings.

Acrobatics from Roderick Thomas of the England Youth Team

Today **Sport**

HOLD THE BACK PAGE!

Working as a soccer journalist can be the most frustrating job in the world. But, as Bob Harris, Chief Football Writer of* Today *newspaper explains, it can also be one of the most exciting – the next best thing to actually being on the pitch.

Just as the ultimate ambition for every professional footballer is to play for his country and every manager to manage his national team, every soccer writer wants to report on the events of his country. I have been lucky and in the past twenty years have had the good fortune to watch England in around 200 games, all over the world. The only games I have missed in that time have been four friendlies.

Exactly like the ambitious footballer or manager, you have to work your way up from the bottom. Most football journalists start on local weekly papers, fetching cups of coffee, running copy and maybe reporting on a local game if he (or she) is lucky. Progress is then usually made through the local amateur teams, semi-professionals and then the big boys from the football league. The higher you go the greater the difficulty in getting in to the games you want to see.

That is especially so for the big games The Football Association stage at Wembley, whether it is a Cup Final or England's international games. Every newspaper in the world wants to send its own reporter to the Cup Final and quite clearly there is not enough room for everyone. The Press Officers at the FA sift through all the applications and sort out those with the greatest merit, starting with the local papers of the teams playing in the final and then moving on to the many national newspapers in the country including my own, *Today*.

Hairy moments

These days it is not simply a question of taking a pencil and notebook to a match. This feature has been written on our Tandy personal computer, which is like a small typewriter with a display screen. When finished it was sent via the telephone to Lancaster Gate, the headquarters of the FA.

Not all grounds are geared up to this latest technology and we have had many hairy moments at foreign grounds. Once we arrived at an Under-21 game in eastern Europe with our phones neatly set out on garden tables under sun umbrellas – the only difficulty was that there was nowhere to connect them!

At an England World Cup match in Poland all the stadium lights were put out while we were still telephoning our copy to London. Without being asked, local lads raced around picking up discarded newspapers, rolling them into torches and setting fire to them so that we could read our stories.

When we went to Albania for the first time we knew from our files that here was an isolated country, suspicious of foreigners (particularly journalists) and without any of the benefits of modern technology. We were allowed only fifty visas to enter Albania for all the writers, radio and television men and we were informed that calls out would be impossible in this 'hostile, unfriendly country'.

What a load of rubbish that turned out to be! Within minutes of arriving at our pleasant hotel we had contacted our offices and we could not have enjoyed a more friendly, warmer welcome from those delightful people of Albania. Mind you, there weren't too many slimline, digital telephones and there were many sore throats on the way home through an excess of shouting down the lines. I managed to be connected to the British Boxing Board of Control instead of my sports desk!

Silly stories

Over the last couple of years, because of a change in newspaper style at the lower end of the market, many of you must think that the press and the players don't talk to each other and that there is no relationship at all between ourselves and the manager.

Fortunately that is not true. There are some silly stories written, quite often by a 'columnist' who sits at home in front of the telly and tries to be clever. But for those of us 'on the road' we can see first hand the problems that arise – how difficult a job the players and manager have in a game which is now world-wide.

I have yet to meet a manager or a player who complained about 'objective' criticism, only when it becomes personal and stupid.

Talking to those involved in the game is an essential part of our work and, for me, one of the most enjoyable aspects. It is extremely educational to listen to experts like Bobby Robson, Don Howe, Bryan Robson, Gary Lineker and the rest. I am particularly lucky as I have had the privilege of writing books with Bobby Robson, Steve Coppell, Graeme Souness, Bruce Grobbelaar and all the England boys.

Most of the time you can relax and talk at your leisure. But these days newspapers demand opinion and 'quotes' from players and coaches immediately after a game and that is not always easy or practicable as we all get ready to rush off to the airport or wherever.

Fortunately places like Wembley have proper

conference rooms but otherwise it means finding people under stands, in dressing rooms, car parks, leaning out of windows or in a restaurant.

Can you imagine how difficult it was when competing with the world's press and television cameras to talk to Diego Maradona, Argentina's captain, after he had knocked England out of the 1986 World Cup with his infamous hand ball and his brilliant solo effort? You couldn't get past his bodyguards!

Greatest thrill

Watching a game of football is a lot easier for us national daily writers. Saturday is a lovely day, when we can relax and enjoy the game, smirking at our Sunday newspaper rivals, knowing we have not got to write our pieces until the next day.

The view of the game at big clubs is usually as good as you can get, high up in the stands in line with the half-way line. It is a much better view than the one from the substitutes' bench where many managers and coaches sit.

However, sometimes you have to survive the elements such as rain on your notebook (as in the open stands in Israel) or the telephone freezing to your ear (as in the depths of a middle Europe winter) or sometimes so far back from the action that we have to debate who scored a goal or made a pass.

The more modern grounds, at least for the big games, not only have facilities for our Tandy machines but sometimes put in television monitors so we see what you are seeing at home.

Not that I would swap. For all the problems it is the greatest thrill in the world to savour the atmosphere of a big game live. To be able to say "*I was there*" and to meet and talk to the heroes of the game afterwards. Add to that the travel, the fun and the company and you can understand why I wake up every day looking forward to the varied work that lies ahead of me.

Maradona's 'goal' against England in the 1986 World Cup

THE REFEREE

...from your local park to Wembley Stadium

Would you like to become a referee? Colin Downey, Referees' Secretary to the FA, explains how the road to Wembley can begin on your local playing field.

Most people would agree that a football match is more enjoyable to play or watch when a qualified referee officiates. Referees are usually former players at school, youth, amateur or, sometimes, professional level.

Basic training is readily available and is provided throughout the country by every County Football Association. Anyone who is interested in becoming a referee does not have to look far to obtain excellent and complete training. Qualified Referee Instructors are waiting to encourage and enrol candidates any time of the year.

Neil Midgley

Keith Hackett

Training courses are usually held one night a week for 6–8 weeks and every football law is discussed in detail. There are 17 Laws of the Game and most time is spent discussing the more important and interesting sections – Law 11 Offside, Law 12 Fouls & Misconduct and Law 13 Free Kicks. At the end of the course an

George Courtney

examination takes place and success is rewarded with a Referee's Certificate and badge. The new referee is graded as Class 3.

After training and qualifying a new referee will start by officiating in local junior football – sometimes youth football, sometimes adult park football. Equally important to gaining experience and practice in a match, referees attend local referees' meetings, organised by The Referees' Association, to discuss problems, seek advice and listen to other referees talk about their experiences. All this forms further training and education which is necessary so that progress can be made to the higher grades, Class 2 and then Class 1.

As a referee gains promotion from Class 3 to Class 1 he may be able to progress from local park football into senior amateur, semi-professional and then, hopefully, professional football. Provided a referee is of the right age it is possible to become a linesman at the top level – the football league – within 8–10 years, but only if the referee works very hard and proves himself to be a good official.

Whilst progress is being made towards the football league there will be many local top league and cup matches to referee and this will include cup finals.

Having reached the football league as a linesman a referee continues to work towards becoming a referee on that league and then even to becoming an international referee on the FIFA list. The last stage involves much travel into Europe and beyond, Real Madrid . . . Juventus . . . the World Cup!

Here in England, in addition to the football league matches, there are also many matches in The Football Association competitions – the FA Youth Cup, the FA Vase, the FA Trophy and the FA Challenge Cup with its final at Wembley Stadium.

Not all referees will reach Wembley, most will be happy to referee the local Cubs' League, Youth League or Saturday/Sunday Leagues.

Refereeing is not easy – fitness, hard work, a general good knowledge and interest in football and, above all, the ability to control the players is necessary. These are some of the reasons why the FA does not allow anyone to qualify as a referee under the age of 14.

It is much better to play football, but one day *you* might wish to become a referee and if you do (or your brother, father, uncle or anyone you know) is interested, full details can be obtained from your own County Football Association or The Football Association, 16 Lancaster Gate, London W2 3LW.

One final thought. As mentioned, refereeing is never easy, so please, as a player do not argue or complain about decisions and as a spectator do not moan at the referee. You never know, one day you might be *the referee!*

Roger Milford

THE ENGLAND

Tony Adams
(Arsenal):

Age 23. In only two full seasons he has played in two Littlewoods Cup Finals, winning in 1987 and captaining the runners-up in 1988, and has established himself in the full England team. Earlier captained the Under-21s (5 caps). Played in eleven of 1988's twelve internationals and achieved the distinction of scoring for both sides in the Holland match at Wembley. Born London.

John Barnes
(Liverpool):

Age 26. He is not always on his best club form for England but did appear in all but one of 1988's internationals. Had a spectacularly successful first season at Anfield, following his £900,000 transfer from Watford, and finished with a League Championship medal and both the PFA and Football Writers' Player of the Year awards. Born Jamaica.

Terry Butcher
(Glasgow Rangers):

Age 31. The big plus of the 1988–89 season for England was his return to the defence after a long absence through injury. Was in Bobby Robson's Ipswich team that won the UEFA Cup in 1981, moving to Rangers for a £750,000 fee in 1986 and captaining his new club to two triumphs in his first season – the Scottish Championship and the Skol Cup. Born Singapore.

Tony Cottee
(Everton):

Age 24. All of his senior England matches have involved coming on as substitute, firstly against Sweden in Stockholm in 1986 when he replaced Steven. West Ham born and bred, he notched 116 goals in 252 first-team matches for the Hammers before his record-breaking £2.2 million move to Everton in 1988. In his debut for his new club he scored a hat-trick against Newcastle.

Tony Dorigo
(Chelsea):

Age 24. Left-back who was in the 1988 squad for the European Championship Finals after playing eleven times for the England Under-21 side. Cost Chelsea their record fee (£475,000) from Aston Villa in 1987, having paid his own fare to fly here for trials from Australia. He could become the first Australian to win full England honours.

SQUAD

The England line-up against Albania in March, 1989

Paul Gascoigne
(Tottenham Hotspur):

Age 22. Gazza won his first full England cap after coming on as substitute for Beardsley for the last five minutes against Denmark in September 1988. Promotion to the senior squad followed thirteen appearances for the England Under-21s and 1988 PFA Young Player of the Year. Was the subject of a £2 million transfer from Newcastle to Tottenham. Born Gateshead.

Mick Harford
(Luton Town):

Age 30. Was Luton's top scorer in the 1987–88 season with twenty-one goals and earned a Littlewoods Cup winner's medal into the bargain. This battling centre-forward won his first cap as a substitute in Israel. Now in his twelfth season with his fifth club, having previously served Lincoln, Newcastle, Bristol City and Birmingham. Born Sunderland.

Steve Hodge
(Nottingham Forest):

Age 27. Was recalled into the England mid-field for the Denmark match in September 1988. Began with Forest, his home-town club, and then had less happy spells with Aston Villa and Tottenham. Unable to settle in London, he returned to Forest in a £575,000 transfer deal in August 1988.

Gary Lineker
(Tottenham Hotspur):

Age 29. England's chief goal-getter in recent times missed the start of the 1989 season following an illness which had no doubt contributed to a disappointing European Championship. Went from Leicester to Everton in 1985 and, after his sparkling 'Golden Boot'-winning show in the 1986 World Cup Finals secured a £2.75 million transfer to Barcelona, where he played under the managership of Johann Cruyff.

Gary Pallister
(Middlesbrough):

Age 24. This 6ft 4in centre-back made an impressive England debut away to Hungary, but his club's involvement in the 1988 end-of-season play-offs cost him a place in the squad for the European Championship Finals. His consolation was to help Boro complete their climb from Division 3 to Division 1 in successive seasons. Born Ramsgate.

Stuart Pearce
(Nottingham Forest):

Age 27. He returned to the England team at left-back for the first four internationals of the 1988–89 season after missing six matches, including the European Championship Finals, with knee trouble. Began his career close to Wembley, with non-league Wealdstone, and joined Forest from Coventry in 1985. Is now their captain.

Bryan Robson
(Manchester United):

Age 32. England's 'Captain Fantastic' has worn the armband with distinction on over 50 occasions and his goal tally places him second behind Lineker among current international players. Cost the then British record fee of £1.5 million in 1981, when he moved from West Bromwich to Manchester United, the club he has captained to two FA Cup Final victories (1983 and 1985). Born Chester-le-Street.

David Rocastle
(Arsenal):

Age 22. He became Bobby Robson's first new cap of the 1988–89 season when he was included against the Danes. He has fourteen caps at Under-21 level, ten of them earned last season when he finished as

THE ENGLAND SQUAD

England's captain in the four-match tournament in Toulon. Plays wide on the right and has scored some spectacular goals for Arsenal. Born Lewisham.

Mel Sterland
(Glasgow Rangers):
Age 28. He made his senior bow in Saudi Arabia in November 1988, after earning seven caps for the Under-21 side and one 'B' honour (with a goal) against Malta. He spent eleven seasons at Sheffield Wednesday before joining Rangers. Born Sheffield.

Gary Stevens
(Glasgow Rangers):
Age 26. Attacking right-back who, in seven seasons' football with Everton, earned League Championship medals in 1985 and 1987, plus honours in two major cup competitions – the FA Cup in 1984 and the European Cup Winners' Cup in 1985. Missed part of the 1986–87 season through injury, but reclaimed his No.2 spot last season. Subject of a £1 million transfer from Everton to Rangers in July 1988. Born Barrow.

Michael Thomas
(Arsenal):
Age 22. Capped at senior level for the first time in Saudi Arabia in November 1988, this attacking full-back or mid-fielder has made a giant leap from reserve team football at Arsenal to the full England team in under two years. Added seven Under-21 caps in 1988 to previous Schoolboy and Youth honours. Born Lambeth.

Peter Shilton

Still England's best goalkeeper at an age when most players have long since hung up their boots, 40-year-old Peter Shilton tells you the secret that has brought him a record number of caps – it's hard work!

"I've always wanted to be number one. But I know I'll only be picked for England if the manager still thinks I can do the job. I've always believed in training hard to stay on the top of my form, even when I was much younger. A goalkeeper depends on his strength, agility and speed of reaction and you have to put yourself through a tough routine nearly every day to keep these skills sharp."

Peter's talent was obvious very early on. He was in Leicester City's first team at 17 and looking so good that the Midlands club were able to let the great Gordon Banks go to Stoke City without any worries. Leicester's confidence was rewarded when Shilton helped them to the 1969 FA Cup Final, at the age of 19. Defeat by Manchester City and relegation in the same season were a big disappointment, but his first England cap came in 1970 and after a period with Stoke City, club success with Nottingham Forest. A key member of Brian Clough's great team of ten years ago, Peter won Championship, League Cup and European Cup medals.

On the international scene, a long and friendly rivalry with Ray Clemence saw Shilton confirmed as England's first choice keeper for the 1982 World Cup in Spain and he has held that position ever since.

Peter's greatest disappointment is that he hasn't yet won an FA Cup winner's medal or a major tournament with England, but who is to say that it might not yet happen. The message to aspiring goalkeepers is that hard work is a must if you want to get to the top – whether you're 14 or 40!

Peter Beardsley

Peter Beardsley has to pinch himself sometimes to be convinced it isn't all a dream. League Championships and Wembley with Liverpool and now an automatic member of the England squad, things have changed a lot since 28-year-old Peter's early years as a professional.

He joined Carlisle United at the age of 18, going to Canada each summer for three years to play for Vancouver Whitecaps. During this period he spent a season at Old Trafford, but didn't get into the first team. Manchester United must have regretted letting him go, as they were prepared to pay £2 million but couldn't prevent him from going to Anfield when Newcastle United finally decided to part with their star player.

It was at Newcastle that Peter's undoubted ability began to be appreciated. Playing alongside Kevin Keegan and Chris Waddle in the team that took the Geordies back to Division 1 brought the best out of him and in January 1986 he was called into the England squad for the first time. A great performance against USSR established Beardsley and Gary Lineker as possibly England's best strikers – something that was proved in the 1986 World Cup Finals in Mexico.

Bobby Robson, the England Team Manager who gave Peter Beardsley his international chance, describes what makes the Liverpool striker so special. *"He's bright, clever, always watching what's going on round him. He has great control, dribbles well, knows when to pass and when to hold on to the ball and he works as hard in defence as he does in attack. Add to that, he's got a great character and is a tremendous member of the squad, whether he's in the team or not. He's a little jewel."*

If a young player is looking for one professional on which to model himself, he need look no further than Peter Beardsley.

Chris Waddle

(Tottenham Hotspur):

Age 29. He became a Newcastle player from non-league Tow Law Town in 1980 and was an England player within five years. His glittering career as an international winger was interrupted in the 1987–88 season by various injury problems, but he is now back to his best form. Tottenham signed him for £590,000 in 1985.

Des Walker

(Nottingham Forest):

Age 24. Quick central defender who made his England debut at senior level as substitute for Tony Adams for the last 25 minutes against Denmark in September 1988. Has played seven times for the Under-21 team and has been a first-team regular at Forest for the past three seasons. Born Hackney, London.

Neil Webb

(Nottingham Forest):

Age 26. Made history as England's 1000th international cap, when he came on as substitute for Hoddle in West Germany in 1987. His father, Doug, was a goal scoring inside-forward with Reading until 1966 and Neil began his career at the same club. Joined Forest from Portsmouth for £250,000 in 1985 and seems destined to become one of the country's top players.

Chris Woods

(Glasgow Rangers):

Age 30. His 6ft 2in frame appeared between the posts for the full 90 minutes in the 1988–89 final European Championship match against USSR and as half-time substitute in the 1989 season's opening international against Denmark. Moved from Norwich to Rangers for a £600,000 fee in 1986. Previously with Nottingham Forest and QPR. Born Boston.

Soccer Knowledge 2

1
What is Gary Lineker's middle name?

2
In 1966 the World Cup was stolen. Who found it?

3
Who was the first substitute to be used in a football league match?

4
In 1924 England first played at Wembley. Who were their opponents?

5
Who invented shin-guards?

6
How many countries entered the first World Cup in Uruguay in 1930?

7
Who was the heaviest player ever to appear for a football league club?

8
In what year did the referee first use a whistle?

9
Which was the first English club to play in a European competition?

10
Where was the first FA Cup Final played?

11
Which country has taken part in the final stages of all thirteen World Cups?

12
Which was the last club to go an entire season without picking up a single point away from home?

13
Who invented the penalty kick?

14
Who was the oldest player to play for England?

15
Name the three sponsors of the Football League Championship.

16
Which club supplied a record seven players for the England team in 1934?

17
Name the first club to be automatically relegated to the GM Vauxhall Conference.

18
Which was the first club to be automatically promoted from the GM Vauxhall Conference?

19
Apart from the inscription, what is the main difference between an FA Cup winner's and runner's-up medal?

20
Where was Terry Butcher born?

21
Where did England last play a full international in England but not at Wembley?

22
Which player has made the briefest appearance for England?

23
Who was the 1000th player to play for England?

24
Have Peter Shilton and Ray Clemence both captained England?

25
Who scored for Brazil against England at Wembley in 1987?

Answers on page 61.

UMBRO –
One of sport's great traditions

Manchester City FA Cup Winners 1934

Sir Stanley Matthews

Bobby Moore lifts the World Cup for England in 1966

Football, fussball, fotboll, soccer . . . however you say it, around the world it's played by more people than any other sport. In Europe, Scandinavia, the Middle East, Australia, the United States of America and Great Britain, many tens of thousands of teams play in kit bearing the distinctive Umbro diamond trade mark.

Umbro International was formed in 1924 by the Humphreys Bros and soon became established as one of the leading football suppliers to both the professional and amateur teams. The brand made its debut in the arena of big sports in 1934 when Manchester City – who still wear Umbro kit today – appeared in the FA Cup Final, and then Sheffield Wednesday in 1935, both winning the coveted silver trophy.

International success

At international level both England and Scotland wear Umbro strips.

The relationships with the Scottish and English Football Associations go back many years and both national teams have experienced their greatest international successes, and some of their most disappointing times it must be said, in the famous white or navy.

It was whilst wearing red shirts, however, that England pulled off the greatest victory in world soccer in 1966 by winning the World Cup. Geoff Hurst scored a memorable hat-trick, the only one ever scored in a World Cup Final, and Nobby Stiles became a fairy-tale figure after his toothy face was seen by millions world-wide doing a dance and jig around the Wembley pitch. The remarkable thing about the '66 World Cup for Umbro was the fact that fifteen of the sixteen teams in the Finals wore Umbro kit, including West Germany, the beaten finalists.

Four years later Umbro helped another team lift the World Cup. This time it was Brazil in Mexico City. Pele, Jarzinho, Rivelino – great names, great players – all associated with Umbro in the World Cup.

England v Scotland 1988

Successful clubs

Umbro over the years has also enjoyed long and harmonious relationships with some of the greatest British clubs and teams. During the early 1960s Tottenham Hotspur became the first club this century to win the FA Cup and First Division Championship double. Blanchflower, Jones and Mackay all wore Umbro. The great teams built by Shankly and Paisley at Liverpool have also donned the Umbro jerseys for many championship-winning occasions, including all their European Cup victories. Hunt, Keegan, Toshack, St. John, Hughes, Thompson . . . the mere mention of their names conjures up excitement – excitement generated with the help of sportswear designed for the job in hand.

The best in the world

And so to today, England and Scotland are still in Umbro kit, as are Manchester City, together with Celtic, Rangers and Aberdeen. In England, Everton, Nottingham Forest, Chelsea, Newcastle, Leeds, Watford, Oxford and many more wear distinctive designs by Umbro. Perhaps Umbro's greatest team of players though was on view in August 1987 when the Rest of the World played a Football League XI as part of the League's Centenary celebrations.

Peter Shilton

Platini, Lineker and Maradona starred and continued Umbro International's link with professional football at the highest level.

When you've got a choice, choose authentic team-wear, footwear and sports balls from the market leaders in soccer – choose Umbro, First for Football!

WELCOME TO

On average, England play four full internationals at Wembley in any one football season. The matches will either be qualifying fixtures in one of the major tournaments like the World Cup or one-off 'friendly' games. But when a visiting national team comes to England, there is little information in the media on where and by whom the team is met, where they stay, when and where they train and what they do in their spare time.

The visitors will have been told the date and venue of the match several months in advance by the FA. Two or three weeks before the big day, they will advise the FA of their exact travel plans in a telex message to Lancaster Gate – the headquarters of the FA, in London. Most teams fly into London's Heathrow Airport, but one or two may come into Gatwick, Luton or Stansted. All visiting teams require a good-sized motor coach (say a fifty-seater) to be put at their disposal, plus a limousine or two for their top officials and a baggage van for all the kit.

The team is usually met by David Barber from the FA Press Office. The limousine will come to Lancaster Gate to pick David up a couple of hours before the team's flight is due to arrive and take him to the airport. He will remain with them for the whole of their stay, with an interpreter if necessary.

When the team arrives, the group coming through customs is always a large one. As well as sixteen players there will be the manager coach, doctor, physio, masseur and several committee officials. Often the Under-21 party will be on the same flight, if they have a match on the evening before the seniors, so that could mean over fifty people in the group altogether.

Once the formalities are over and the party

Wembley Stadium

OUR VISITORS

16 Lancaster Gate, London – the FA's HQ

officially welcomed to England by the FA, they will be led away to the transport waiting outside the airport terminal. Surprisingly, this generally takes only a few minutes – unless somebody has lost a bag, which creates a minor panic. It can be serious if it has a player's boots in it!

Whether the visiting team is a famous one like Brazil or a smaller one like Turkey, they are put up at the first-class Royal Garden Hotel in Kensington, with its central location next to Hyde Park and close to London's main shopping centres. The coach journey from the airport will only have taken about thirty minutes, but it will probably take the same length of time for everyone to be checked in to the hotel.

Most of the arrangements for the team will have been planned well in advance. Meal times will be known and times for training sessions and free periods for sightseeing in the coach or local shopping. If a team has arrived on the Monday before a Wednesday night match, which is customary, they will train on Monday evening, Tuesday morning and Tuesday evening. It would be most unusual for anyone to train on the day of the match.

The Monday session, under lights at a non-league ground like Hendon or Hounslow, will be a 'loosener' after the journey. On Tuesday morning, at the playing fields of the Bank of England Sports Club at Roehampton, there will be a lot more running about, with plenty of shooting practice and probably an eight-a-side game too. Tuesday evening means a trip to Wembley to check the dressing rooms and test out the pitch with a few set-pieces. We have to allow the visitors on the pitch, even though the big match is only twenty-four hours away, because we would expect the same facility when the England team goes abroad.

There is tremendous pre-match excitement at the hotel when the players come down from their rooms and walk out to the coach in their tracksuits. The reception area suddenly fills up with journalists, supporters and friends of the players. The usual time for leaving is 6.00 p.m. and the ride to Wembley, with a police escort, will take anything from thirty minutes to an hour, depending on the traffic.

On arrival at the huge gates to the famous Wembley 'tunnel', the players file through the opening and hand their dressing-room passes to a Wembley official. There is always a large congregation of fans cheering wildly for England, which has to be controlled by police on horseback, and a few moments later the likes of Gary Lineker and Bryan Robson will be seen stepping down from the England coach which has just arrived from the team's headquarters in Buckinghamshire.

In about an hour's time the match will start. Afterwards there will be interviews in the press room or in the 'tunnel' itself. Then it's back to the hotel in the coach for some dinner, ecstatic or subdued – depending on the result!

WORLD CUP 1930-1986

The FIFA World Cup, awarded since 1974

International sides have competed in thirteen World Cup Finals since the first tournament was played in 1930. Here's a recap of the highlights of those competitions as we build up to the 1990 Finals this summer in Italy.

1930: Uruguay

Uruguay staged the first World Cup tournament in 1930. Thirteen countries took part, including only three from Europe – probably because in those days European teams would have had to undertake a two-week sea voyage. The hosts were undoubtedly favourites to win, and this they achieved, defeating Argentina 4–2 in an exciting final. The following day was proclaimed a national holiday. The golden 50,000 franc cup, designed by the French sculptor Lafleur, had been handed to Uruguayan captain Nasazzi by Jules Rimet.

1934: Italy

Still annoyed that so many of the top European teams had declined to travel to South America in 1930, and also suffering from a players' strike at home, Uruguay decided to boycott the second tournament, played in Italy in 1934. Once again the host country won the final. Orsi's 82nd-minute equaliser forced extra time against Czechoslovakia and Schiario's goal won it for the Italians 2–1.

1938: France

Some sceptics had suggested that the Italians could only win on home soil, but they were proved wrong when Italy retained the trophy, beating Hungary 4–2 in the 1938 Final in Paris.

1950: Brazil

The 1950 World Cup, now known officially as the 'Jules Rimet Trophy', took place for the second time in South America – in Brazil. Once again there were defections and withdrawals, but this time England competed. Enthusiasm for the game in Brazil was at a fanatical level and it was a pity that the immense three-tiered Maracana Stadium – the largest in the world with a 200,000 capacity – had not been completed when the tournament started. Uruguay's 2–1 victory over Brazil in the final brought the World Cup back to Montevideo after a gap of twenty years.

1954: Switzerland

Hungary had been hot favourites to win in the Swiss finals in 1954, and the great question before the final was whether the legendary Ferenc Puskas would recover from his ankle injury in time to play. Hungary had already beaten Germany 8–3 in one of the group matches, but, even with Puskas, they went down to a shock 3–2 defeat in the final. It was Hungary's first defeat in thirty international matches.

1958: Sweden

Played in Sweden, the 1958 World Cup was notable for the emergence of the 4–2–4 system of play and the explosive talent of a 17-year-old phenomenon called Pele. Sweden met Brazil in the final and the Swedes took the lead after only four minutes. Brazil refused to panic, as many had predicted they would, and were level within six minutes. Brazil's scorers in their eventual 5–2 victory were Vava (twice), Pele (twice) and Zagalo.

1962: Chile

Brazil retained the World Cup in 1962. They had been favourites to beat Czechoslovakia in the final in Santiago. Amarildo's cunning cross-shot immediately equalised Masopust's 16th-minute opener, and then Brazil went into their shell for a while, before striking after 69 minutes with a headed goal by Zito.

FINALS

The Jules Rimet Trophy, awarded between 1930 and 1970, now belongs to Brazil for having won the World Cup Final three times in 1958, 1962 and 1970

Schroif, perhaps blinded by the sun, dropped Santos' high ball into the goalmouth and Vava took advantage of the slip to make the final score 3–1.

1966: England

The 1966 World Cup was the first since 1934 to be won by the home side. It was a World Cup full of controversy, persisting long after the dramatic final thanks to the shot on the turn by West Ham United's Geoff Hurst which struck the underside of the bar and came down either on the line or just behind it. (The English players nearest to the incident and, more importantly, the Russian linesman Bakhramov, said it was a goal.)

England won a superb final against West Germany 4–2 after extra time, and Hurst became the first player to register a hat-trick in a World Cup Final. The Jules Rimet Trophy had at last come to the country where football began.

1970: Mexico

The 1970 finals took place in Mexico. As a continuation of the trend which had seen the host country do well in the last three tournaments – Sweden finalists (1958), Chile semi-finalists (1962) and England winners (1966) – Mexico got through to the last eight. But Italy ended the hopes of the Mexicans, winning 4–1 in Toluca. 800 million watched the final between Brazil and Italy on television. Brazil won convincingly 4–1.

1974: West Germany

The 1974 final in the Munich Olympic Stadium, between Holland and West Germany, refereed by Jack Taylor from Wolverhampton, produced three goals, two of them from the penalty-mark. Before half-time West Germany had slipped into an ultimately unassailable 2–1 lead. So the host country had won again.

Brazil, as three-time winners (1958, 1962 and 1970) had won the Jules Rimet Trophy outright. A new trophy of solid gold, 36 centimetres high and known as the 'FIFA World Cup', was designed by an Italian from an entry of some 53 submitted for selection and was used in 1974 for the first time.

1978: Argentina

The second winners of the new trophy were Argentina in 1978. The hosts had won for the fifth time in World Cup history, beating Holland 3–1 in the final.

For the third time the final went into extra time, after Dutch substitute Nanninga's header had cancelled out Kempes' opening goal for Argentina. Valencia-bound Kempes scored their second in extra time and Bertoni clinched victory with a third.

1982: Spain

The 1982 finals were held in Spain, and Italy, the eventual winners, began the tournament in a very low-key fashion, drawing all three group matches and scoring only twice. But the team which had failed to beat Cameroon picked up in the second round, and their 3–2 victory against Brazil – Rossi got a hat-trick – was probably the most exciting match of the finals. Italy won the World Cup for the third time, thereby emulating Brazil, by virtue of a 3–1 win against West Germany in Madrid's Bernabeu Stadium.

1986: Mexico

The only countries with 100 per cent records after the first round were Brazil and Denmark, and both were fancied to reach the final. But Brazil lost to France after a tense penalty shoot-out in the quarter-final and Denmark inexplicably lost their form to go down 5–1 to Spain in the second round.

Argentina had ended England's World Cup dreams for another four years, as Diego Maradona weaved his magic in the quarter-final, and they went on to confront West Germany, who were aiming to become the first Europeans to win a final on the American continent, in the magnificent Aztec Stadium. The resilient Germans fought back to equalise from 2–0 down, but Maradona then provided the defence-splitting pass from which Burruchaga fired home the winner with six minutes left.

WORLD CUP

Italy 1990

ITALIA '90

Bari, Della Vittoria Stadium

Genoa, Luigi Ferraris Stadium

Bologna, Renato Dell'Ara Stadium

Milan, Giuseppe Meazza Stadium

Cagliari, Sant'Elia Stadium

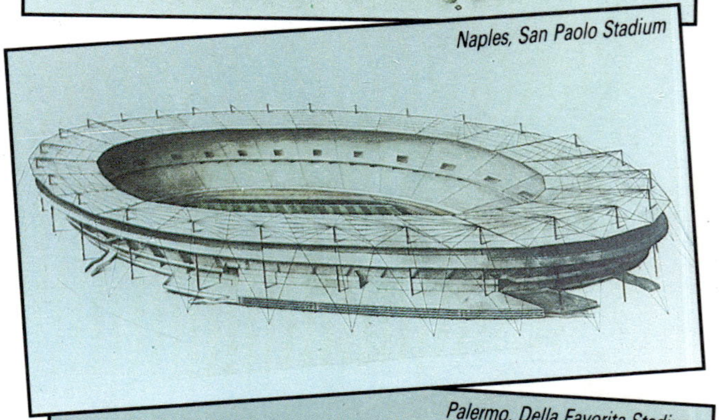

Naples, San Paolo Stadium

Florence, Comunale Stadium

Palermo, Della Favorita Stadium

FINALS

Italy are hosts to the fourteenth World Cup Finals this summer and work to make the various grounds superb pitches to play on has been underway since 1987.

Each of the twelve grounds has undergone a massive facelift, and the combined capacity of the grounds is a staggering 696,000 – but this figure will be minute compared to the millions who will watch the matches on their TV sets. More people will see the 1990 World Cup Finals than at any other time in the history of the competition, thanks to the arrival of satellite television. The photographs on these pages are artists' impressions of what each stadium should look like.

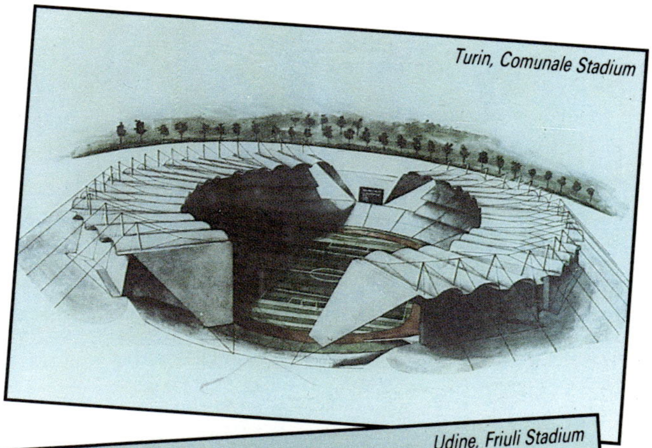
Turin, Comunale Stadium

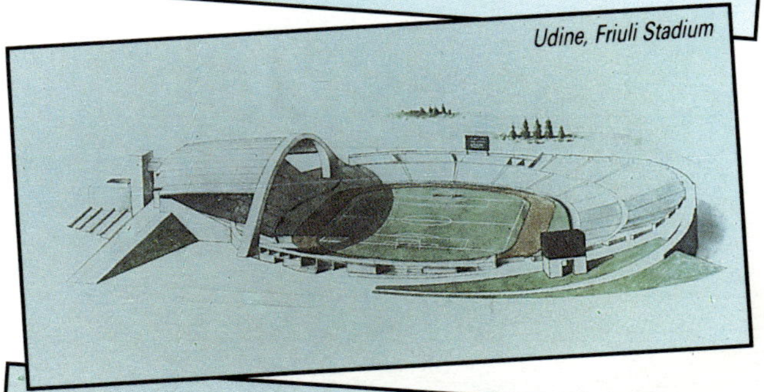
Udine, Friuli Stadium

Verona, Comunale Stadium

Rome, Olimpico Stadium

THE GROUNDS

City	Stadium	Capacity	Population	Nearest airport
Bari	Della Vittoria	52,000	362,000	Palese (12km)
Bologna	Renato Dell'Ara	46,000	432,000	Guglielmo Marconi (6km)
Cagliari	Sant'Elia	45,000	222,000	Elmas (7km)
Florence	Stadio Comunale	61,000	425,000	Pisa Peretola (4km)
Genoa	Luigi Ferraris	44,000	727,000	Cristoforo Colombo (7km)
Milan	Giuseppe Meazza	87,000	1.5 million	Linate (10km)
Naples	San Paolo	80,000	1.2 million	Capodichino (7km)
Palermo	Della Favorita	41,000	724,000	Punta Raisi (32km)
Rome	Stadio Olimpico	83,000	2.8 million	Leonardo da Vinci (36 km)
Turin	Stadio Comunale	70,000	1 million	Citta di Torino (18 km)
Udine	Friuli	43,000	100,000	Trieste (40km)
Verona	Stadio Comunale	44,000	259,000	Villafranca (12km)

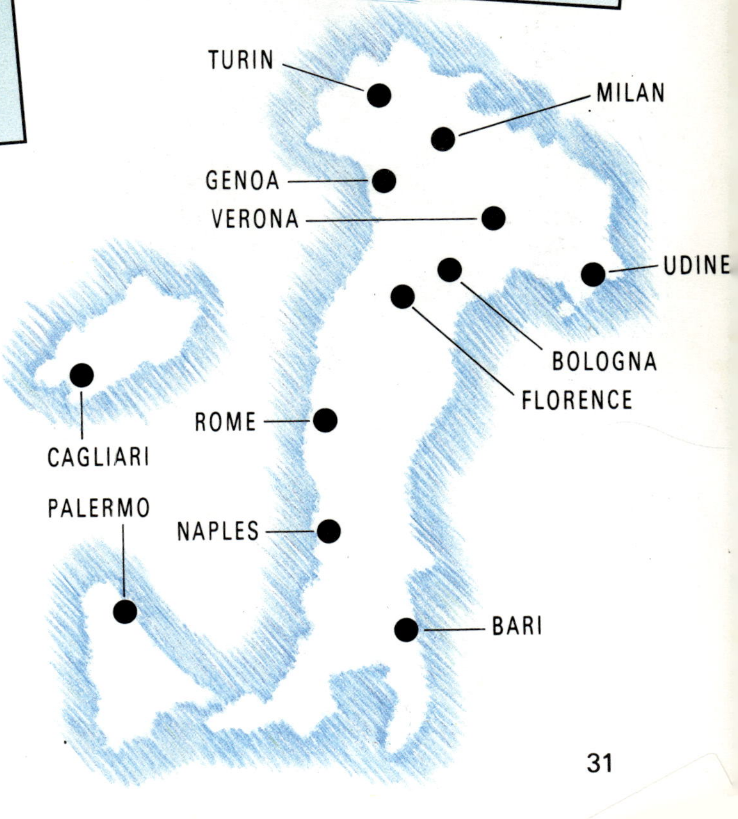

WORLD CUP
Final Score

Chart the progress of all the teams in the 1990 World Cup Finals. The draw for the First Round matches is in December 1989 and each of the 24 teams has been given a number. Write the teams against their numbers below and the details of the First Round matches on the chart opposite. Then use the chart to keep track of the 52 matches throughout the competition.

1	13
2	14
3	15
4	16
5	17
6	18
7	19
8	20
9	21
10	22
11	23
12	24

ENGLAND'S RESULTS IN THE FINALS

1930 Did not compete
1934 Did not compete
1938 Did not compete
1950
Pool II
England 2 Chile 0
United States 1 England 0
Spain 1 England 0
1954
Pool IV
England 4 Belgium 4
England 2 Switzerland 0
Quarter-Final
Uruguay 4 England 2
1958
Pool IV
England 2 Russia 2
England 0 Brazil 0
England 2 Austria 2
Play Off
Russia 1 England 0
1962
Group IV
Hungary 2 England 1
England 3 Argentina 1
England 0 Bulgaria 0
Quarter-Final
Brazil 3 England 1
1966
Group I
England 0 Uruguay 0
England 2 Mexico 0
England 2 France 0
Quarter-Final
England 1 Argentina 0
Semi-Final
England 2 Portugal 1
Final
England 4 West Germany 2
1970
Group III
England 1 Rumania 0
Brazil 1 England 0
Czechoslovakia 0 England 1
Quarter-Final
West Germany 3 England 2
1974 Did not qualify
1978 Did not qualify
1982
Group IV
England 3 France 1
England 2 Czechoslovakia 0
England 1 Kuwait 0
Second Round
Group B
West Germany 0 England 0
Spain 0 England 0
1986
Group F
Portugal 1 England 0
England 0 Morocco 0
England 3 Poland 0
Second Round
England 3 Paraguay 0
Quarter-Final
Argentina 2 England 1

FIRST ROUND

Group	Date	Match	Venue
GROUP A	Sat, June 9	1 v 2	Rome
	Sun, June 10	3 v 4	Florence
	Thu, June 14	1 v 3	Rome
	Fri, June 15	2 v 4	Florence
	Tue, June 19	1 v 4	Rome
	Tue, June 19	2 v 3	Florence
GROUP B	Fri, June 8	5 v 6	Milan
	Sat, June 9	7 v 8	Bari
	Wed, June 13	5 v 7	Naples
	Thu, June 14	6 v 8	Bari
	Mon, June 18	5 v 8	Naples
	Mon, June 18	6 v 7	Bari
GROUP C	Sun, June 10	9 v 10	Turin
	Mon, June 11	11 v 12	Genoa
	Sat, June 18	9 v 11	Turin
	Sat, June 18	10 v 12	Genoa
	Wed, June 20	9 v 12	Turin
	Wed, June 20	10 v 11	Genoa
GROUP D	Sat, June 9	15 v 16	Bologna
	Sun, June 10	13 v 14	Milan
	Thu, June 14	14 v 16	Bologna
	Fri, June 15	13 v 15	Milan
	Tue, June 19	13 v 16	Milan
	Tue, June 19	14 v 15	Bologna
GROUP E	Tue, June 12	17 v 18	Verona
	Wed, June 13	19 v 20	Udine
	Sun, June 17	17 v 19	Verona
	Sun, June 17	18 v 20	Udine
	Thu, June 21	17 v 20	Verona
	Thu, June 21	18 v 19	Udine
GROUP F	Mon, June 11	21 v 22	Cagliari
	Tue, June 12	23 v 24	Palermo
	Sat, June 16	21 v 23	Cagliari
	Sun, June 17	22 v 24	Palermo
	Thu, June 21	21 v 24	Cagliari
	Thu, June 21	22 v 23	Palermo

SECOND ROUND

Sat, June 23	match in Naples
Sat, June 23	match in Bari
Sun, June 24	match in Turin
Sun, June 24	match in Milan
Mon, June 25	match in Rome
Mon, June 25	match in Genoa
Tue, June 26	match in Bologna
Tue, June 26	match in Verona

QUARTER-FINALS

Sat, June 30	match in Rome
Sat, June 30	match in Florence
Sun, July 1	match in Naples
Sun, July 1	match in Milan

SEMI-FINALS

Tue, July 3	match in Naples
Wed, July 4	match in Turin

THIRD PLACE MATCH

Sat, July 7 match in Bari

FINAL

Sun, July 8 match in Rome

MATCHES			SCORES			FINAL GROUP TABLES

	v			:	
	v			:	
	v			:	
	v			:	
	v			:	
	v			:	

	P	W	D	L	Pts
1					
2					
3					
4					

	v			:	
	v			:	
	v			:	
	v			:	
	v			:	
	v			:	

	P	W	D	L	Pts
1					
2					
3					
4					

	v			:	
	v			:	
	v			:	
	v			:	
	v			:	
	v			:	

	P	W	D	L	Pts
1					
2					
3					
4					

	v			:	
	v			:	
	v			:	
	v			:	
	v			:	
	v			:	

	P	W	D	L	Pts
1					
2					
3					
4					

	v			:	
	v			:	
	v			:	
	v			:	
	v			:	
	v			:	

	P	W	D	L	Pts
1					
2					
3					
4					

	v			:	
	v			:	
	v			:	
	v			:	
	v			:	
	v			:	

	P	W	D	L	Pts
1					
2					
3					
4					

						WINNERS
	v			:		
	v			:		
	v			:		
	v			:		
	v			:		
	v			:		
	v			:		
	v			:		

	v			:		
	v			:		
	v			:		
	v			:		

	v			:		
	v			:		

	v			:		

	v			:		

Soccer Knowledge 3

1
Which team has won the European Cup the most times?

2
Which team has won the League Championship the most times?

3
Two clubs both have grounds called St. James Park. Who are they?

4
If the Rams were playing at The Dell, what match would you be watching?

5
Which was the first English club to win the European Cup?

6
Ronald Koeman and Ruud Gullit are international stars. For which country?

7
Which was the second English team to win the European Cup?

8
With which club did Gary Lineker start his career?

9
If the Dons were at home to the Hammers, which London derby would you be watching?

10
When Platini and Beckenbauer were on opposite sides during an international match who would be playing?

11
Whose home is the Baseball Ground?

12
Chris Waddle and Paul Gascoigne both played for which north-east club prior to joining Tottenham?

13
With which club did Diego Maradona win an Italian League Championship medal?

14
Which was the third English team to win the European Cup?

15
Where is the FA's National School for promising 14-year-old players?

16
Were FA Cup matches once decided over two legs?

17
If a team travelled from Kenilworth Road to play at Loftus Road, which two teams would be playing?

18
Name the Argentinian who scored a classic goal for Spurs in the 1981 FA Cup Final replay.

19
Eusebio was a star player for which country?

20
Stanley Matthews, after many attempts, finally won an FA Cup winner's medal with which club?

21
Which player was the first to miss a penalty in an FA Cup Final at Wembley?

22
Name the first goalkeeper to save an FA Cup Final penalty at Wembley.

23
Who was the first English £1 million footballer?

24
Which famous pop star supports Watford?

25
Derek Dougan, John Richards and Steve Bull have all scored goals for which famous club?

Answers on page 61.

WEMBLEY

Some of the greatest sporting events in the footballing world are played at one particular stadium. Each year it hosts the finals of our home competitions and it is the dream for many a player to represent the England international side on its famous turf. The stadium is, of course, Wembley. Martin Corrie, Wembley's Press Officer, reports.

England matches always hold a special thrill for everyone at Wembley, for the Stadium has been England's permanent home since 1966 and the England *v* Scotland fixture goes way back to 1924. That first game between the two countries at Wembley ended in a 1–1 draw and in fact was only the second fixture to be played at what was then known as the Empire Stadium.

The first fixture is unlikely ever to be forgotten, for an estimated 200,000 fans saw Bolton Wanderers beat West Ham United 2–0. But of course the game nearly didn't happen at all. Half an hour after it was due to kick off almost the entire pitch was covered with spectators but then that magnificent white horse called Billie appeared and his rider, PC George Scorey, slowly but surely moved back the fans to around the touchline.

Wembley's proudest England moment was on 30th July 1966. West Ham's Geoff Hurst became the first player to score a hat-trick in a World Cup Final and fellow Hammer, Bobby Moore, led England to a dramatic and most emphatic 4–2 victory over West Germany. The Germans have played at Wembley on a number of occasions, but each season brings the opportunity to see new opposition – as well as the excitement from teams such as the magical Brazilians, the skilful Italians, or the brilliance of the Dutch.

STADIUM

In 1988, Colombia played at Wembley for the first time, and those of us privileged to see the game enjoyed what was probably one of the most entertaining England games of all time. 1989 saw a fascinating tussle with Albania in April, followed a month later by the first visit from Chile.

Every match at Wembley is a major operation. Teams of specialists behind the scenes meet up well in advance to carefully plan each game. Everything from ticket sales to the medical teams, from security to the groundsman and his dedicated team who lovingly tend the hallowed turf.

Next time you see a great England game at Wembley, spare a thought for the cashiers, the catering staff, the box office and a whole host of others busy inside the depths of the great stadium. They can hear the roar of the crowd very well, but the view from their offices leaves rather a lot to be desired!

FOOTBALLING COUNTRIES of the world

Football is probably the world's most popular sport. But who plays where, when, and in what colour strip? Check the facts for 135 of the world's footballing countries in this table.

Country	National stadium	Capacity	Colours (shirts/shorts)	Duration of season
Albania	Qemal Stafa, Tirana	19,000	all red	Sept–May
Algeria	Olympic, Algiers	80,000	green/white	Sept–June
Angola	Coqueiros	14,000	red/black	April–Jan
Antigua	Rec. Gnd, St John's	25,000	gold/black	Aug–Dec
Argentina	River Plate, Buenos Aires	76,000	sky blue & white/ black	March–Dec
Australia	National Ath. Stadium Bruce, ACT	25,000	amber/green	March–Oct
Austria	Prater, Vienna	70,000	white/black	Aug–June
Bahamas	Thomas A. Robinson	15,000	yellow/black	Oct–May
Bahrain	Isa Town Stadium	16,000	white/red	Oct–June
Bangladesh	Dacca Stadium	55,000	orange/white	Apr–Dec
Barbados	National, Waterford	12,000	royal blue/gold	Jan–May
Belgium	Heysel, Brussels	62,000	all red	July–June
Benin	Cotonou II Stadium	7,000	all green	Nov–June
Bermuda	National, Prospect	10,000	royal blue/white	Sept–April
Bolivia	Nat. Olympic, La Paz	55,000	green/white	April–Dec
Brazil	'Maracana', Rio De Janeiro	200,000	yellow/blue	Jan–Dec
Bulgaria	'Wassil Levski', Sofia	70,000	white/green	March–Dec
Burma	Aung San Memorial Stadium, Rangoon	45,000	red/white	May–April
Cameroon	Ahmadou Ahidjo Stadium, Yaounde	50,000	green/red	Oct–Aug
Canada	Olympic, Montreal	64,000	all red	May–Nov
Central Africa	Barthelemy Boganda, Bangui	35,000	grey-blue/white	Oct–July
Chile	National, Santiago	74,000	red/blue	Feb–Dec
China (P.R.)	Beijing Workers'	63,000	red/white	March–Nov
Colombia	'El Campin', Bogota	57,000	red/blue	Feb–Dec
Congo	Revolution Stadium, Brazzaville	50,000	all red	May–Dec
Costa Rica	National, Explanada De La Sabana	30,000	red/blue	March–Oct
Cuba	Juan Abrantes, Havana	18,000	white/dark blue	July–Nov
Cyprus	Makarion Ath. Centre, Nicosia	20,000	blue/white	Oct–June
Czechoslovakia	Strahov, Prague	60,000	red/white	Feb–Nov
Denmark	Idraetspark, Copenhagen	48,000	red/white	April–Nov
Dominican Republic	'Juan Pablo Duarte', Domingo Santo	30,000	navy blue/white	March–Dec
Ecuador	Modelo, Guayaquil	49,000	yellow/blue	March–Dec
Egypt	Nasser Stadium, Cairo	100,000	red/white	Sept–June
England	Wembley, London	87,000	white/navy blue	Aug–May
Ethiopia	Addis Ababa Stadium	30,000	green, yellow & red/yellow	Sept–June
Fiji	National Sports	25,000	white/black	March–Sept

Country	National stadium	Capacity	Colours (shirts/shorts)	Duration of season
Finland	Olympic, Helsinki	50,000	white/blue	April–Oct
France	Parc Des Princes, Paris	50,000	blue/white	July–June
Gabon	President Bongo Sports Complex, Libreville	30,000	blue, yellow & green/blue, yellow & green	Oct–July
Gambia	Box-Bar, Banjul	10,000	all white	Nov–July
Germany (East)	Central, Leipzig	95,000	white/blue	Aug–June
Germany (West)	Olympic, Berlin	80,000	white/black	Aug–June
Ghana	Accra Sports Stadium	34,000	all white	Jan–Nov
Greece	Karaiskaki, Athens	42,000	white/blue	Sept–June
Grenada	Queen's Park, St George's	8,000	green & yellow/ red	July–Dec
Guatemala	Mateo Flores Stadium, Guatemala City	50,000	all white	Jan–Dec
Guinea	28th September Stadium, Conakry	40,000	red & white/ yellow & white	Oct–June
Guyana	Georgetown Cricket Club, Bourda	15,000	all green	March–Dec
Haiti	Sylvio-Cator Stadium	25,000	black & red/ black	Nov–May
Honduras	Norte-A-Sur Stadium, Tegucigalpa	50,000	white/blue	Feb–Dec
Hong Kong	Government Stadium, Sookunpoo	28,000	red/white	Sept–June
Hungary	Nep, Budapest	71,000	red/white	Aug–June
Iceland	Laugardalsvollur Stadium, Reykjavik	15,000	blue/white	May–Oct
India	New Delhi Stadium	40,000	white & sky blue/white	Jan–Dec
Indonesia	Senayan, Jakarta	110,000	red/white	Jan–Dec
Iran	Azadi Stadium, Tehran	100,000	green/white	April–Feb
Iraq	Sha'ab, Baghdad	50,000	all white	Oct–May
Ireland (Northern)	Windsor Park, Belfast	50,000	green/white	Aug–May
Ireland (Rep. of)	Lansdowne Road, Dublin	48,000	green/white	Aug–May
Israel	Ramat-Gan Stadium	55,000	blue/white	Sept–June
Italy	Olympic, Rome	90,000	blue/white	Sept–June
Ivory Coast	Houphouet Boigny Stadium, Abidjan	27,000	orange/white	Nov–Aug
Jamaica	Independence Park, Kingston	40,000	green/black	Aug–April
Japan	National, Tokyo	62,000	all white	April–Jan
Jordan	Amman Int. Stadium	30,000	all white	April–Dec
Kenya	City Stadium, Nairobi	18,000	red, green & white/red, green & black	Feb–Oct
Korea (North)	Moranbong Stadium, Pyongyang	90,000	all white	March–Nov

Country	National stadium	Capacity	Colours (shirts/shorts)	Duration of season
Korea (South)	Seoul Municipal	30,000	all red	March–Nov
Kuwait	Kuwait Sporting Club	25,000	blue & white/ white	Oct–May
Laos	National, Vientiane	11,000	red/white	Nov–May
Lebanon	Camille Chamoun Stadium, Beirut	60,000	red/white white	Oct–June
Lesotho	National Stadium, Maseru	20,000	blue, white & green/white	Nov–Oct
Libya	Tripoli Sports City Stadium	70,000	green & white/ white	Oct–May
Liechtenstein	Nation, Vaduz	10,000	blue/red	Aug–July
Luxembourg	Municipal Stadium	15,000	red/white	Aug–June
Macao	Sports Stadium	12,000	red & green/ white	Oct–June
Madagascar	Mahamasina Municipal Stadium, Tananarive	14,000	red/white	Nov–Oct
Malawi	Kamuzu, Blantyre	53,000	all red	March–Dec
Malaysia	Jalan, Kuala Lumpur	37,000	yellow/black	Jan–July
Mali	Omnisport, Bamako	30,000	green/yellow	Oct–June
Malta	Ta'Qali Stadium	40,000	red/white	Sept–May
Mauritania	National Stadium, Nouakchott	6,000	green & yellow/ blue	Nov–July
Mauritius	George V, Curepipe	20,000	red/white	Sept–June
Mexico	Aztec, Mexico City	108,000	green/white	Sept–June
Morocco	Stadium of Honour, Casablanca	70,000	all red	Sept–June
Mozambique	Machava, Maputo	35,000	red/black	Sept–June
Nepal	Dasarath Rangasala	35,000	all red	April–Nov
Netherlands	Olympic, Amsterdam	60,000	orange/white	Aug–June
Netherlands Antilles	Korsouw Sports Centre	12,000	white red & blue/white	Jan–Dec
New Zealand	Mt. Smart, Auckland	18,000	all white	March–Oct
Nicaragua	National, Managua	30,000	blue & white	June–Sept
Niger	National, Niamey	7,000	orange/white	Oct–July
Nigeria	National, Lagos	50,000	green/white	Jan–Dec
Norway	Ullevaal Stadium, Oslo	25,000	red/white	April–Nov
Pakistan	Karachi Stadium	86,000	green/white	Jan–Dec

Country	National stadium	Capacity	Colours (shirts/shorts)	Duration of season
Papua New Guinea	Sir Hubert Murray, Port Moresby	20,000	red/black	Feb–Nov
Paraguay	'Defensores Del Chaco', Asuncion	60,000	red & white/blue	March–Nov
Peru	National Stadium, Lima	45,000	white with red stripe/white	April–Dec
Philippines	Rizal Memorial Stadium, Manila	30,000	blue & red/blue	July–April
Poland	10th Anniversary Stadium, Warsaw	87,000	white/red	March–Nov
Portugal	National, Lisbon	51,000	red/green	Sept–July
Qatar	Khalifa Olympic Stadium, Doha	40,000	white/maroon	Sept–June
Rumania	23rd August Stadium, Bucharest	95,000	yellow/blue	Aug–July
Saudi Arabia	King Fahd Int. Stadium, Riyadh	70,000	green & white/ white	Oct–Feb
Scotland	Hampden Park, Glasgow	70,000	dark blue/white	Aug–May
Senegal	Dempa Diop, Dakar	15,000	green/yellow	Oct–July
Sierra Leone	Brookfields Stadium, Freetown	36,000	green, white & blue/white	May–Dec
Singapore	National, Kallang	65,000	all red	June–Oct
Somalia	CONS, Mogadiscio	15,000	sky blue/white	Nov–March
Spain	Nou Camp, Barcelona	120,000	red/blue	Sept–June
Sri Lanka	Sugathadasa Stadium, Colombo	25,000	maroon & gold/ white	Aug–Feb
Sudan	Khartoum Stadium	30,000	green/white	July–June
Surinam	National Stadium, Paramaribo	21,000	red, green & white/white	March–Dec
Sweden	Solna Stadium	52,000	yellow/blue	April–Oct
Switzerland	Wankdorf, Berne	60,000	red/white	Aug–June
Syria	Al-Abassiyne Stadium, Damascus	45,000	all white	Sept–June
Taiwan	Taipei Municipal	30,000	blue/white	Jan–Dec
Tanzania	National Stadium, Dar-Es-Salaam	3,000	yellow & black/ yellow	Sept–Aug
Thailand	Suphachalasai Stadium, Bangkok	45,000	all red	Nov–April
Togo	Etienne Eyadema	20,000	white/green	Oct–July
Trinidad & Tobago	Queen's Park Oval, Port of Spain	25,000	red/black	June–Dec
Tunisia	Olympic, Tunis	50,000	red/white	Sept–June
Turkey	19th May, Ankara	35,000	all white	Sept–June
Uganda	Nakivubo Stadium, Kampala	35,000	yellow & black/ black	Jan–Nov
Uruguay	Centenary Stadium Montevideo	74,000	sky blue/black	March–Dec
USA	—	—	white/blue	April–Sept
USSR	Lenin, Moscow	100,000	red/white	April–Nov
Venezuela	Olympic, Caracas	25,000	dark red/white	Jan–Dec
Vietnam SR	Hang Day, Hanoi	40,000	red/white	Nov–May
Wales	Ninian Park, Cardiff	40,000	red/white	Aug–May
Yemen PDR	National Stadium	10,000	light blue/white	Oct–April
Yemen AR	Al Habashie, Aden	4,500	all green	Sept–May
Yugoslavia	Red Star, Belgrade	95,000	blue/white	March–Dec
Zaire	May, Kinshasa	60,000	green/yellow	Feb–Nov
Zambia	Independence Stadium, Lusaka	30,000	green & copper/ white green black & red	March–Nov

BEFORE THE

What was it like for the England squad of the last century when they were preparing for an international? And what is it like for today's players?

The England squad that played in the international against Scotland at Richmond, 1893

Squad preparation ...ancient

Around the time of the first international match in 1872, the best club sides in England and Scotland were Wanderers and Queen's Park (Glasgow) respectively. The officials of these two clubs had met in February of that year and had decided to ask the Committee of The Football Association to choose eleven players to represent England. The selected team would go to Scotland to do battle against a similar number of Scotsmen under the laws provided by the Committee.

Of the England team originally chosen, four players were unable to play for various reasons, while Scotland for their part could not obtain the services of two of their star players. The England players lived so far apart that it was impossible for them to get together for practice games, and the weather in Scotland proved fatal to the success of the attempts at practice made by the Scotsmen.

Most of the English team arrived in Glasgow on the Friday night and took up their quarters at Carrick's Royal Hotel. Four players were unable to leave London until Friday evening and had to travel through the night. Two o'clock had been fixed as the kick-off time, and both teams were ready and raring to go, but a start was not made until 2.20 p.m. The watching crowd increased as the game progressed and every available portion of the ground was filled before the end. The English team wore white jerseys, with the arms of England embroidered on the left breast. (To this day the England players' jerseys are predominantly white, although a red and navy blue trim features in the current *Umbro* design.)

MATCH

... and modern

Nowadays there is much preparation for matches by the team. Where once the England players used to travel overnight on cold, uncomfortable trains, finally arriving at the ground by horse-drawn carriage just before the kick-off, and with no tactical plan in defence or attack beyond the simple desire to win, there is now a more scientific approach. Squads gather together three or four days before an international match; there are training sessions and team meetings which help to produce a sense of team-spirit within the national side; the horse and carriage has given way to twentieth century progress, and when England teams travel abroad they now span the earth, hopping from country to country in luxury aircraft, with the eyes of the football world upon their every movement.

The selection of the teams to represent England was originally carried out by The Football Association Council, but the increase in the number of members on the Council made it necessary for a Selection Committee to be appointed, and in 1888 the original committee of seven members was duly elected. This committee continued to have a large say in choosing the England team until the 1960s, when Alf Ramsey, the first 'team manager' as we understand the term nowadays, merely 'informed' them of his selection.

ENGLAND CAPS

The style of the England cap has hardly changed over the years. This cap was awarded for the European Championship qualifying match in Turkey in 1987

Football is a game rich in tradition, and one of the best known of all practices is the giving of special caps to players who have been in international matches. But what is the background to this rather odd custom?

The idea of the England 'cap' belongs to N.L. Jackson, a famous Old Corinthian on the FA Committee. At a meeting held at Kennington Oval in 1886, his proposal was carried:

"That all players taking part for England in future international matches be presented with a white silk cap with red rose embroidered on the front. These to be termed 'International Caps'."

The first cap was actually of royal blue velvet, with a rose at the front and the date of the match on the peak. Later on the initial letter of the opposing country, *e.g.* 'S' for Scotland, was added on the peak; then came a silver tassel; then the rose was replaced by the three lions. Today's caps, still in blue velvet, are supplied to the FA by the Midlands-based firm Toye Kenning & Spencer. One cap is awarded for an appearance in a one-off Friendly International and one cap (*only one*) is awarded for a competition like the World Cup or the European Championship. So a player could have appeared in all the qualifying matches and all the matches in the final tournament – perhaps a dozen matches altogether – and yet only receive one cap.

THE SOCCER

If you play or watch football – we'll make you a Soccer Star

The Soccer Star Scheme is an exciting new soccer education programme developed by The Football Association.

Test your soccer ability on the six Soccer Star challenges – if you reach the 6 Star Grade The Football Association will recommend you for a trial at your local football league club.

The Soccer Star Scheme is open to all boys and girls between 6–16 years of age interested in improving and enjoying their football.

You can join the Soccer Star Scheme by asking your teacher, club manager, youth leader or at your local sports centre.

On completion of every course you will receive a sportsmanship booklet, a certificate, badges, letter from the England manager and a personal computer graph.

THE COCA-COLA FOOTBALL ASSOCIATION SOCCER STAR SCHEME

This is to Certify that

Paul Brown

has successfully completed a course of instruction in the age range Under 16 of

Pennywell School

and is awarded

R.W. ROBSON
NATIONAL COACH

How do you measure up to the Soccer Star Scheme?

RUNNING WITH THE BALL

John Barnes

▲ In a channel, 30 yards long and 2 yards wide, can you beat John Barnes' score from start to finish of *3.8 seconds*?

TURNING

John Barnes

Can you perform your favourite turn 3 times quicker than *10 seconds*? ▶

STAR SCHEME

THE COCA-COLA FOOTBALL ASSOCIATION SOCCER STAR SCHEME

CHAMPION CLASS

To improve your soccer skills:

★ ask your teacher/coach about the Soccer Star Scheme

★ read the Soccer Star Book (Collins £2.95)

★ view the Soccer Star Video (CBS £9.99)

HEADING

Bryan Robson

▲ Can you head the ball into goal 3 times out of 3 if it is thrown to you?

- for 7 and 8 year olds, 2 yards from goal.
- for 9 and 10 year olds, 6 yards from goal.
- for 11 year olds and over, 12 yards from goal.

Competition

Win the chance to interview Bobby Robson and ask him any questions of your choice. To enter, write to Bobby Robson (at the address below) and tell him **in not more than 12 words** how the Soccer Star Scheme has improved your football skills. Closing date for entries is 1 March 1990.

Send your entry to:
Bobby Robson,
Soccer Star Scheme
The Football Association
22/24A The Broadway
Darkes Lane
Potters Bar, Herts.

Remember: no more than 12 words!

DRIBBLING

Peter Beardsley

▲ How quickly can you dribble the ball in front of 4 markers?

SHOOTING

Bryan Robson

◀ From a spot 3 yards into the penalty area can you shoot a moving ball into the far corner of the goal 3 times with your right foot and 3 times with your left foot?

How quickly can you run around 4 markers?
▼

SPEED

Bryan Robson

Training in progress

STARS

Have you ever wondered if England players are born or created? Is their talent natural or is it the result of good training? At the FA's National School in rural Shropshire, a handful of carefully picked schoolboys are put through a vigorous training programme, designed to make them the soccer stars of the future.

The Football Association's National School, installed at Lilleshall, Shropshire, since 1984, is the realisation of much planning and thought aimed at improving the standard of English football at the highest level. The idea for the School originated in a document co-authored by the FA's National Coach, Bobby Robson, and Assistant National Coach, Charles Hughes, called *"The Blueprint for the Achievement of Excellence"*.

The School was officially opened by HRH The Duke of Kent, the FA's President, at a special ceremony on 4th September 1984 with officials present from the FA and General Motors (the sponsor of the School), along with the first batch of twenty-five young pupils and their parents. To reflect the sponsor's generous contribution, the School's full title is the "GM Vauxhall Football Association National School".

The boys at the School, 14 years old when they start, are undoubtedly some of the football stars of the future. They are able to reap the benefit of receiving instruction and advice from some of the game's top coaches, while at the same time devoting a proper proportion of their time to their academic studies. The boys receive their normal education at Idsall School, just five miles from Lilleshall Hall. The boys live at the Hall and take advantage of the first-class facilities provided by the Sports Council at this National Sports Centre.

Dave Sexton, the Technical Director at Lilleshall

OF THE FUTURE

Dave Sexton is the National School's Technical Director and is responsible for organising the boys' football timetable. Dave is always struck by their tremendous enthusiasm, something he puts down to their love of the game. He is one of the game's most astute coaches and has managed successful club sides in the First Division (Chelsea, Manchester United and Coventry City), as well as currently managing the England Under-21 team.

Probably the most important change in the boys' routine, in football terms, has been their removal from the physical and mental grind of playing in up to six matches a week for school and club sides. These boys only play in up to thirty matches a season against professional clubs' youth teams. Time made available for coaching has been put to good use, with the emphasis on developing the boys' individual skills. The School is a successful venture already, with several "graduates" having made their football league debuts and one having even made the England Under-21 team.

Two years after the opening of the National School the FA's National Rehabilitation and Sports Injury Centre was established, also at Lilleshall. This has already become recognised as the National Centre for the rehabilitation and treatment of sports-related injuries and has been used by many top professional footballers.

The Rehabilitation Centre has now been expanded to include a Human Performance Department whose aim is to assess the fitness of footballers (and people from other sports) and provide guidance on appropriate training programmes. These technical initiatives by the FA are significant because a player's career is shortened when he becomes injured. Speed of recovery is important, but the completeness of the recovery is even more vital.

HRH The Duke of Kent and officials from the FA at the National School's opening in September, 1984

Training game for the stars of the future

Soccer Knowledge 4

1
Who scored a hat-trick for England in the 1966 World Cup Final?

2
Who has scored the most goals for England?

3
Who was the manager of the England World Cup winning team of 1966?

4
Which player has scored England's quickest World Cup goal?

5
Have England ever lost a World Cup match to America?

6
Who is the youngest player ever to play for England at Under-21 level?

7
In what year did Peter Shilton make his England debut?

8
Who managed England before Bobby Robson?

9
How many goals did Gary Lineker score in the 1986 World Cup Finals?

10
When England won the World Cup in 1966, what colour shirts were they wearing?

11
Did Ray Clemence play in goal for England whilst a Tottenham Hotspur player?

12
Did Alan Smith represent England at both senior and non-league level?

13
What is the colour of England's third choice kit?

14
Who was in goal for England in the 1966 World Cup Final?

15
Which two countries competed in the world's first international match?

16
Have Brazil ever won the Rous Cup?

17
How many lions are there on the England crest?

18
Which was the last European country England needed to play in order to have played them all?

19
Have England ever reached the final of the European Championships?

20
Have England ever won the European Championship for Under-21 teams?

21
Have England ever scored nine goals against Scotland in one match?

22
Have England ever scored nine goals against Wales in one match?

23
Which player scored a hat-trick against England in the 1988 European Championship?

24
Name the last brothers to play for England.

25
Have England ever beaten Brazil in Brazil?

Answers on page 61.

AS SEEN

The first football match to be broadcast in England was broadcast on radio. This was the First Division match between Arsenal and Sheffield United at Highbury, in 1927. In that same year the match between Corinthians and Newcastle United was the first FA Cup tie to be broadcast. For many years there were almost continuous arguments about allowing important football matches to be broadcast – and at different times both the FA and the League have banned broadcasting.

Whereas the FA agreed to the televising of certain matches, the spread of television since World War II was not at first met with open arms by the League. An agreement made in 1960 to screen a number of league matches had to be scrapped after some of the leading clubs had refused to take part. But in 1964, BBC2

A rocket similar to the one which will launch BSB's satellite

The BSB satellite

ON TV

Watching a football match on television is taken for granted these days. All the big games are screened and most of them are shown live. The future for armchair soccer now comes in the shape of a BSB satellite receiving dish or "squarial", but things were very different when football was first broadcast.

was allowed to screen an edited 45-minute version of one league game per week.

The first FA Cup Final at which any part of the game was televised was the 1937 Final between Sunderland and Preston North End. In the post-war era the first final to be televised from start to finish was Charlton Athletic against Burnley in 1947. Now, of course, the whole of the FA Cup Final is seen live every year – not only in Britain but in about seventy other countries world-wide (live or shown later).

England's matches have been covered extensively since the 1950s. Of those who heard it, who could forget Kenneth Wolstenholme's commentary for the BBC at the World Cup Final in 1966? As England's hat-trick hero Geoff Hurst received a long pass upfield from skipper Bobby Moore in the dying seconds and started to bear down on the West Germans' goal, Wolstenholme noticed that one or two supporters were already on the pitch by the far touchline. "They think it's all over," he said, and as Hurst went on to shoot left-footed past Tilkowski for England's fourth goal, he continued: "It is now." Those words are remembered by millions who watched the match at home on that magical day. They have become part of football folklore for England.

All of England's away matches these days are soon to be shown live on BSB (British Satellite Broadcasting) and all home matches at Wembley, too. When they are especially important and a capacity crowd is expected they may also be shown on the BBC. There were millions of bleary-eyed viewers during the 1986 World Cup Finals in Mexico, when England's matches were televised live from Monterrey and Mexico City's Aztec Stadium at a time when most people are tucked up in bed.

The satellite revolution has brought a huge benefit to the game and fans – how we watch and enjoy football on television will never be the same again. In August 1988, British Satellite Broadcasting and the BBC announced a major five year deal worth £30 million with The Football Association.

As a result of this deal, FA Cup matches and the cream of international football will soon be seen on BSB's Sports Channel. BSB will also introduce live cup football on Saturday evenings as well as live England matches and live FA Cup replays mid-week. Football lovers will enjoy much more in the way of in- depth coverage, including interviews and match reviews because BSB will dedicate a whole channel to sport.

In May 1989, BSB added to this a £12.25 million deal for three years with the Scottish FA and Scottish League.

Thanks to satellite TV, football coverage will continue to improve and the money generated has helped secure the sport's future. As they say at BSB, "It's smart to be square!"

Soccer Wordsearch

Hidden in the square below are 47 familiar words from the world of soccer. Some are written forwards, some backwards and others diagonally or up and down. You may use letters more than once.

All 47 words are listed here. How many can you find? The solution can be found on page 61.

Home
FA Cup
Net
Spurs
League
QPR
Liverpool
Ball
Coach
Kick Off
Corner
Shoot
Fan
Pass
Bar
Soccer
Away
Post
Gunners
Italy
Nil
Tackle
Lineker
Robson
Pele
Brazil
Penalty
Man Utd
Hurst
Final
Cross
Star
Rous Cup
Header
Lancaster Gate
Wembley
Victory
Foul
Draw
Save
World Cup
Goal
Platini
Boss
Shilton
Lineup
Flag

F	A	N	T	S	O	P	S	K	I	C	K	O	F	F	W
A	W	I	T	A	L	Y	E	C	L	F	F	A	R	O	O
C	A	L	I	N	E	U	P	N	O	E	I	L	A	U	R
U	Y	S	H	I	L	T	O	N	A	R	A	N	A	L	L
P	E	L	E	M	A	N	U	T	D	L	N	G	A	G	D
N	B	H	G	U	N	N	E	R	S	L	T	E	U	L	C
E	H	O	M	E	O	W	E	M	B	L	E	Y	R	E	U
T	C	C	S	P	L	A	T	I	N	I	L	A	O	G	P
S	T	R	K	S	R	O	B	S	O	N	W	S	A	V	E
P	S	O	R	O	U	S	C	U	P	E	O	O	B	D	I
U	R	S	H	E	A	D	E	R	L	K	O	V	R	E	Y
R	U	S	L	A	N	C	A	S	T	E	R	G	A	T	E
S	H	O	O	T	S	O	C	C	E	R	O	U	Z	I	W
S	S	A	P	C	O	A	C	H	S	T	A	R	I	R	A
V	I	C	T	O	R	Y	T	A	C	K	L	E	L	A	R
Q	P	R	L	O	O	P	R	E	V	I	L	L	A	B	D

S.A.F.E.

Soccer As Family Entertainment

Soccer, as we all know, is a spectator sport for the whole family. The Football Association and The Football Trust are funding a special project called SAFE – Soccer As Family Entertainment – which aims at introducing young fans and their families to the national game. John Maiden, the project co-ordinator of SAFE explains.

Until a few years ago most football league clubs did not make special provision for family spectators. But the situation has changed quite dramatically during the 1980s as more and more of the game's administrators have become aware of the need for young fans to be introduced to spectatorship in a secure and friendly atmosphere.

It is quite true that many grounds have a long tradition as friendly, cheerful places to be on a Saturday afternoon. After all, football supporters need to have a good sense of humour on occasions, to cheer each other up when their team is failing to win or to play entertaining football. The people you watch the game with can contribute to your enjoyment of the occasion, and the 1988–89 season, in particular, saw an upsurge in good humour, with many clubs parading mascots, and producing inflatable emblems in response to the initiative taken by their fans in bringing a sense of fun to our national game. However, it is now recognised in most quarters that in addition to the loyal fans who will continue to follow their team, no matter what its league position, there is a need to encourage new fans. Obviously, a successful team, playing good football, will always attract a few more 'fair-weather' supporters than during its less effective spells, but because football, by its very nature, is all about winning and losing, not all clubs can enjoy equally good results on the field.

Fortunately, for clubs and fans alike, there is one area of the game in which everyone can win. This aspect involves the comfort and safety of spectators on match-days, and the extent to which the football club can serve its local community the rest of the week.

Match-day provision includes creating special areas for families, juniors, the disabled, the elderly, etc. At some clubs this means Family Club rooms for refreshments and entertainment before and after the game, as well as a Family Enclosure from which to watch the game. It may also mean that there is an opportunity for social and/or sporting contact with groups of visiting families or junior fans – thereby helping to remove the need for rigid segregation at grounds. Many schools are offered free or reduced-price admission to selected matches, and the opportunity to provide ball-boys and girls.

At other times, schools may be offered visits by players to answer questions, show videos or give coaching demonstrations. The ground itself may be available for tours and other activities for special groups, such as Junior Supporters.

The Family Enclosure at Wembley on the day of the 1988 Charity Shield match

A letter or phone call to your local club should provide details of what is on offer where you live. If you have difficulty in obtaining information on a particular club write to: SAFE, The Football Association, 16 Lancaster Gate, London W2 3LW. Details of Wembley's Family Enclosure may also be obtained from this address. Enquiries for Wembley Stadium Tours should be directed to Wembley Stadium Ltd. (tel. 01-902 8833).

FIFA'S
Fair Play Campaign

Since 1904 the Fédération Internationale de Football Association (better known as FIFA) has been the world governing body of football. Over the years FIFA has dealt with some important points which affect the game of football, and one of the most vital in recent years has been the theme of 'fair play'.

It was at the 46th FIFA Congress, held in Zurich in 1988, that fair play was presented to FIFA's 166 member countries. The General Secretary of FIFA, Joseph S. Blatter, said that the new fair play campaign would be the first act in a long-term plan for guidance and education, resulting in a better image for football and sport in general.

At the congress, FIFA distributed yellow cards printed in seven different languages, each calling for fair play. The cards are shown on this page. The idea of the card is quite simple: it is meant to be used playfully in everyday situations as an appeal for fair play amongst players and officials at football clubs all over the world. And in the long-run, the message of fair play should reach out to today's youth in all corners of the earth.

Fair Play means

- ★ keeping to the rules of the game
- ★ acting in a law-abiding way
- ★ showing respect for an opponent
- ★ admitting your own faults
- ★ showing good character
- ★ being a good loser – and a winner, too

BUDGET RENT A CAR - *Supporters of football*

Celebrating the England squad's sponsorship by Budget Rent A Car

Budget Rent A Car supports the England Football Team in a very practical way – by sponsorship. Whenever a new England player is capped, Budget presents him with the keys to a Ford XR3i, a car whose sporty image is in line with that of the players. Recent recipients include Mel Sterland, Dave Seaman, Michael Thomas, and Des Walker.

Budget takes an interest in both national and local sporting events. The company's International Headquarters are at Hemel Hempstead, and in addition to its sponsorship of the England squad, it also sponsors the local football team. In fact Budget has a policy of promoting excellence in young athletes in general. Olympic swimmers Sharron Davies and Nick Gillingham are just two of the people the company has helped recently.

With over 3,400 outlets in 120 countries and a fleet size of some 175,000 vehicles, Budget Rent A Car is the largest franchised car rental network in the world. It can therefore provide a comprehensive service for the international traveller, with a wide range of travel and leisure programmes. In the UK, Budget has 133 outlets, with a total fleet size of over 10,000 vehicles. In the past year, its UK Car Rental fleet alone has travelled a distance equivalent to a journey to the sun and back! However, the company's fleet is constantly updated, and all its cars are less than four months old.

Budget is involved in a wide range of charitable activities, many of which include guest appearances by football celebrities. A Saloon Car Championship sponsored by the company was held at 14 venues throughout the country during 1989. Budget also organised a variety of events for Comic Relief's "2nd Red Nose Day" in March 1989.

One recent event arranged by Budget was an All Stars Charity Football Match between the Hemel Hempstead team it sponsors and an England ex-International Squad. The match not only served as an encouragement for the local football team (who won!), it also raised funds for The Guide Dogs For The Blind Association. In line with its image as a caring yet dynamic company, Budget will continue to support and promote charities and sports events in the future.

SOCCER

the world of football photography

Who sits behind the long lens at football matches? And what does it take to get those all-action soccer shots? Monte Fresco, sports photographer with the Bob Thomas Sports Photographic Agency, takes us behind the scenes.

Football and 31-year-old Bob Thomas are indivisible. His famous Northampton-based firm of photographers was founded in 1975, when Bob was only 17 years of age. Bob now employs a staff of six photographers, ranging from the youngest, 22-year-old Shaun Botterill to the oldest, 53-year-old Monte Fresco.

Bob Thomas enjoys an enviable world-wide reputation and is regularly called upon by football governing bodies to advise on photographic arrangements for such huge events as the World Cup, the European Championship and major domestic league matches.

The agency covers all types of sport, but Bob Thomas is *the* football specialist, averaging approximately fifty first class matches every season.

Award-winning cameraman Bob has covered all of the England team internationals both at home and abroad for the last ten years. His very first was the England *v* Wales match at Wembley in 1973 when he was still only 14! Bob's first foreign international was to Luxembourg in 1977 for the day, leaving home at 5 a.m. and returning just before midnight.

Bob numbers amongst his friends many past and present top players, and his football photographs adorn the walls of their homes. The England manager, Bobby Robson, in particular has been a great help and influence, allowing Bob on the team's bus, both to and from training sessions and even matches, letting him take 'special' pictures in the Wembley dressing room, and even on one memorable occasion giving him

Top. France's Patrick Battiston clashes with Brazil's Careca in the 1986 World Cup Quarter Final

Centre. In the Friendly Match between England and Aylesbury United, June 1988, England's Chris Waddle takes on the Aylesbury goalkeeper, Tim Garner

Bottom. Brazil fans cheer their side in the 1986 World Cup Finals

SHOTS

permission to sit on the team bench during an international match!

With the World Cup in Italy in 1990, Bob and his team are heavily involved in travelling the globe to ensure that the agency has action, portraits and team groups of all 24 qualified nations. The agency will then be able to supply the whole of the football world with the pictures of the 24 qualifying countries well before the teams reach Italy.

This is the third World Cup that the organisation has covered in this way, ensuring that magazines, newspapers, TV stations, books and other publications around the world are supplied with the very best and up-to-date high quality colour pictures of the teams competing.

Getting these pictures has not always been easy. Senior Photographer, Dave Rogers, was sent to cover the Algeria *v* Nigeria World Cup qualifier in Constantine and was waiting to follow the players onto the pitch when the Nigerians stopped, produced a live chicken and commenced to slaughter it – for good luck! A stunned Dave tried to concentrate on taking his match pictures, like a good professional, but admits he was delighted when Algeria won the match – so much for good luck!

Another photographer, Clive Brunskill, was even arrested in the line of his photographic duty! Clive was sent to Damascus in 1985 to cover the World Cup qualifying match Syria *v* Iraq and was promptly arrested at passport control. One of the stipulations of entering the country at that time was that you had to have 100 US dollars in cash and produce this money at passport control! He was only released when a representative of the hotel where he was staying was contacted. The representative paid the 100 dollars, Clive was released, covered the match (a draw) and then the hotel charged him an extra 100 dollars for all the trouble he had caused them! But for Clive the adventure was not yet over. During his stay he contracted food poisoning. Although in agony he covered the match and left the country in a wheelchair – being pushed by Joao Havelange, the President of FIFA, across the tarmac.

Next time you see the name 'Bob Thomas' on a football picture, I hope that you will spare a thought for the photographers who sit on wet, windy, sunny, hot or cold football pitches around the world. And after reading this, at least you may know who some of them are.

Top. England captain, Bryan Robson, at the Lilleshall National Sports Centre

Centre. Argentina's Diego Maradona is fouled by South Korea's Jung-Moo Huh in the 1986 World Cup Finals

Bottom. In the match against Morocco in the 1986 World Cup Finals, England's Bryan Robson injured his shoulder in this incident with Morocco's Bixaz

Did you know?

Floodlights
England first played under floodlights in a match against the United States in New York in 1953. Two years later the lights were switched on at Wembley near to the end of England's match with Spain when the fog came down.

Fastest goal
England's fastest goal was Bill Nicholson's after 19 seconds of the match against Portugal at Goodison Park in 1951. Bryan Robson's opener against France in the 1982 World Cup came after 27 seconds.

North Korea
North Korea is the only country which has played a full international on English soil but has never played against England. The Koreans played four World Cup matches here in 1966 – against USSR, Italy, Chile and Portugal.

Albania
When England met Albania in a World Cup qualifying match in March 1989, it was possible to say that England had then played every European country which had a full international team.

Brothers
Bobby and Jackie Charlton appeared in the same England team on 28 occasions. The only two brothers before them to play together for England as professionals were Frank and Frederick Forman of Nottingham Forest in the 1890s.

Down under
Australia has never sent its full international team to play in England, although organised football in that country dates from the 1880s. But England has been 'down under' more than 20 times for internationals and test matches, most recently in 1983.

Midweek attendance
The record attendance for a midweek match in England – 100,000 – was set when England played Argentina at Wembley in 1951. It has since been equalled on a number of occasions.

Most caps
Only four players in history have won over 100 caps for England. Bobby Moore has the most (108), closely followed by Bobby Charlton (106), Billy Wright (105) and Peter Shilton (105 by April, 1989).

Biggest wins
England's record victory in a full international is 13–0 against Ireland in Belfast in 1882. There were 10–0 wins against Portugal (1947) and the United States (1964) and an 11–1 win against Austria (1908). An amazing 17–0 scoreline against Australia in 1951 was achieved in a match not classed as a full international.

Youngest captain
England's youngest ever captain is Bobby Moore, who led the team against Czechoslovakia in Bratislava in 1963 at the age of 22. It was the West Ham United half-back's 12th international.

Team managers
England has had five team managers: Walter Winterbottom (1946–62), Alf Ramsey (1963–74), Don Revie (1974–77), Ron Greenwood (1977–82) and Bobby Robson (from 1982). Joe Mercer assumed the role of 'caretaker manager' for seven internationals in May/June 1974.

Substitutes
The International FA Board decided in 1932 to allow substitutes in international matches if previously agreed by both teams. Jimmy Mullen of Wolverhampton Wanderers became the first substitute to score for England, against Belgium in 1950. England's first substitute to be used in a World Cup match was Tommy Wright, who replaced the injured Keith Newton against Rumania in Guadalajara (1970).

Youngest and oldest
Manchester United's Duncan Edwards was 18 when he played against Scotland in 1955. Leslie Compton of Arsenal was 38 years old when he made his England debut against Wales in 1950.

Shortest and tallest
The shortest goalkeeper to play for England was Davison of Sheffield Wednesday, against Wales in 1922. He was 5 feet 7 inches tall. Joe Corrigan, who kept goal in 9 internationals, was 6 feet $4\frac{1}{2}$ inches.

Goal grabbers
Steve Bloomer, an inside-forward dedicated to the task of scoring goals, got 28 in 24 internationals for England. Nat Lofthouse, 'the Lion of Vienna', managed 30 in 33 post-war internationals. Bobby Charlton has scored the most goals for England, with 49.

Pitch and wicket
More than a dozen men have made international appearances for England in both football and cricket. Denis Compton, Arsenal outside-left and Middlesex batsman, played in eleven war-time soccer internationals and made the first of 78 Test appearances in 1937.

Non-league player
The first professional to appear for England while on the books of a club outside the football league was Joe Baker of Hibernian, first capped against Yugoslavia in 1960.

For and against
Stanley Mortensen made 25 post-war appearances in full internationals for England and on one occasion played *against* England. He was reserve for England against Wales in 1943 and came on for Wales' injured left-half Powell.

Unbroken run
In all internationals for England, Billy Wright set up a world record with a run of 70 consecutive appearances – beginning with the match against France in 1951 and ending with that against the United States in 1959.

Amateur players
The last amateur to appear in a full international for England was Bernard Joy, centre-half against Belgium in 1936. England last fielded eleven amateurs in a full international against Wales in 1895.

Gunners for England
Arsenal had seven players in the England team against Italy at Highbury in 1934: Moss, Male, Hapgood, Copping, Bowden, Drake and Bastin.

Wolves at the back
Wolverhampton Wanderers provided England's half-back line against USSR (twice), Brazil and Austria in 1958. The players were Eddie Clamp, Billy Wright and Bill Slater.

Crowd-puller
The British record attendance of 149,547 was set when England played Scotland at Hampden Park, Glasgow in 1937.

Unique surname
Derek Ufton is the only player ever to have played for England whose surname begins with the letter 'U'. He was capped once in the mid-1950s and his league side was Charlton Athletic.

ENGLAND *Who's Who* COMPETITION

This is your chance to win a trip to England's training headquarters at Bisham Abbey. See the stars train! Get all their autographs! Then watch them play in a big international at Wembley!

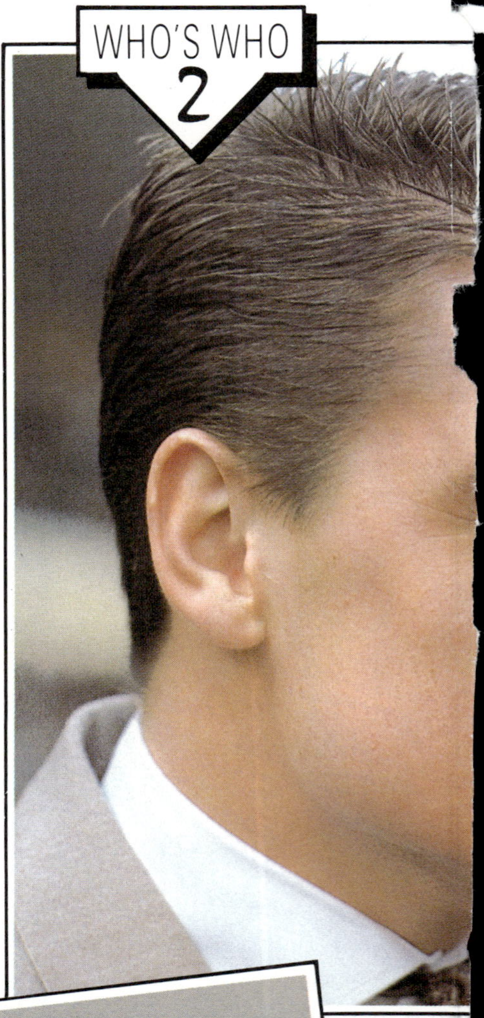

All you have to do is look at Bob Thomas' three great *A Question of Sport* photographs. Then:

1. Name the three players
2. Say which were their first matches for England
3. Say with which clubs they started their football league careers

Complete the entry form on the opposite page and send it to the address shown before 1st March 1990.

The readers sending the first three correct answers to be drawn on 1st March 1990 will win this trip-of-a-lifetime for themselves and one parent or friend.

ENGLAND WHO'S WHO COMPETITION ENTRY FORM

Write your answers in the spaces provided

Who's Who 1

His name is ....

His first match for England was ....

His first football league club was ....

Who's Who 2

His name is ....

His first match for England was ....

His first football league club was ....

Who's Who 3

His name is ....

His first match for England was ....

His first football league club was ....

Your name........................ Age ....

Address...

....

All entry forms should be returned to the following address:
England Who's Who Competition
Editorial Department
World International Publishing Limited
P.O. Box 111
Great Ducie Street
Manchester M60 3BL

Don't forget! The closing date is 1st March 1990.

Diary

OF FOOTBALL EVENTS 1990

JANUARY

6 FA Challenge Cup 3rd Round
17 Littlewood Cup 5th Round
27 FA Challenge Cup 4th Round

FEBRUARY

7 INTERNATIONAL DATE
14 Littlewood Cup Semi-Final (1st Legs)
17 FA Challenge Cup 5th Round
28 Littlewoods Cup Semi-Final (2nd Legs)

MARCH

7 European Cups Quarter-Finals (1st Legs)
10 FA Challenge Cup 6th Round
21 European Cups Quarter-Finals (2nd Legs)
28 INTERNATIONAL DATE

APRIL

4 European Cups Semi-Finals (1st Legs)
7 FA Challenge Cup Semi-Finals
18 European Cups Semi-Finals (2nd Legs)
25 INTERNATIONAL DATE (provisional)
29 Littlewoods Cup Final (provisional)

MAY

2 UEFA Cup Final (1st Leg)
5 End of the Football League Season
9 European Cup Winners' Cup Final
12 FA Challenge Cup Final
15 INTERNATIONAL DATE (ROUS CUP)
16 UEFA Cup Final (2nd Leg)
22 INTERNATIONAL DATE (ROUS CUP)
23 European Champion Clubs' Cup Final

JUNE

8 FIFA World Cup Finals begin

JULY

8 FIFA World Cup Finals end

Bryan Robson and Gary Lineker

Paul Gascoigne

Soccer Knowledge

ANSWERS

Peter Beardsley

GAME 1

1. Plymouth Argyle
2. Santos
3. Cardiff City
4. Berwick Rangers
5. Queens Park Rangers, in 1981
6. Fulham
7. Hove
8. Sunderland
9. Sheffield Wednesday *v* Wolverhampton Wanderers
10. Coventry City, in 1987
11. Watford *v* Brentford
12. Liverpool
13. Norman Whiteside, 17 years 42 days
14. Luton Town *v* Northampton Town
15. Paul Allen, 17 years 256 days
16. Manchester City
17. Leeds United
18. Barcelona
19. Norwich City *v* Crystal Palace
20. No
21. Twelve yards
22. Crystal Palace and Charlton Athletic
23. a) Yes b) No
24. Notts County, established in 1862
25. Italy

GAME 2

1. Winston
2. A dog called Pickles
3. Keith Peacock for Charlton Athletic, in 1965
4. Scotland (1–1)
5. Samuel Widdowson, in 1874
6. Thirteen
7. William Foulke, 25 stone
8. 1878, in a match at Nottingham Forest
9. Birmingham City, in 1955
10. Kennington Oval, in 1872
11. Brazil
12. Nelson, in 1930–31
13. Irish Football Association
14. Stanley Matthews, 42 years
15. Canon, *Today*, Barclays Bank
16. Arsenal
17. Lincoln City, in 1987
18. Scarborough, in 1987
19. The winners' medals are heavier
20. Singapore
21. Goodison Park, Everton, in 1973
22. Phil Neal, 30 seconds, in 1982 against France
23. Neil Webb, 1987 against West Germany
24. Yes
25. Mirandinha

GAME 3

1. Real Madrid
2. Liverpool
3. Newcastle United and Exeter City
4. Southampton *v* Derby County
5. Manchester United, in 1968
6. Netherlands
7. Liverpool, in 1977
8. Leicester City
9. Wimbledon *v* West Ham United
10. France and West Germany
11. Derby County
12. Newcastle United
13. Napoli, in 1987
14. Nottingham Forest, in 1979
15. Lilleshall, in Shropshire
16. Yes
17. Queens Park Rangers *v* Luton Town
18. Ricardo Villa
19. Portugal
20. Blackpool, in 1953
21. John Aldridge, in 1988 for Liverpool
22. Dave Beasant, in 1988 for Wimbledon
23. Trevor Francis, in 1979
24. Elton John
25. Wolverhampton Wanderers

GAME 4

1. Geoff Hurst
2. Bobby Charlton, 49 goals
3. Alf Ramsey
4. Bryan Robson, 27 seconds, in 1982 against France
5. Yes, in 1950
6. Lee Sharpe, 17 years 8 months, in 1989 against Greece
7. 1970, against East Germany
8. Ron Greenwood
9. Six
10. Red
11. Yes
12. Yes
13. Sky Blue
14. Gordon Banks
15. Scotland and England
16. Yes
17. Three
18. Albania
19. No, not yet!
20. Yes, twice, (1982 and 1984)
21. Yes, in 1961, 9–3
22. Yes, in 1896, 9–1
23. Marco van Basten, for Holland
24. Bobby and Jackie Charlton
25. Yes, 2–0 in 1984

How many did you score?

Some questions were easier than others, and some you might have found impossible to answer! But how good is your soccer knowledge really? Check here to see if you're a goal-grabber or just a reserve.

0– 10 What's the view like from the stands?
11– 20 Stay on the sub's bench!
21– 30 Do you like scoring own goals?
31– 40 Sorry, take an early bath.
41– 50 Looks like you're playing downhill.
51– 60 Your transfer fee is going up.
61– 70 Is their goalie a friend of yours?
71– 80 You must have golden boots!
81– 90 Ever been on *A Question of Sport*?
91–100 A real medal-winning champion!!

Wordsearch

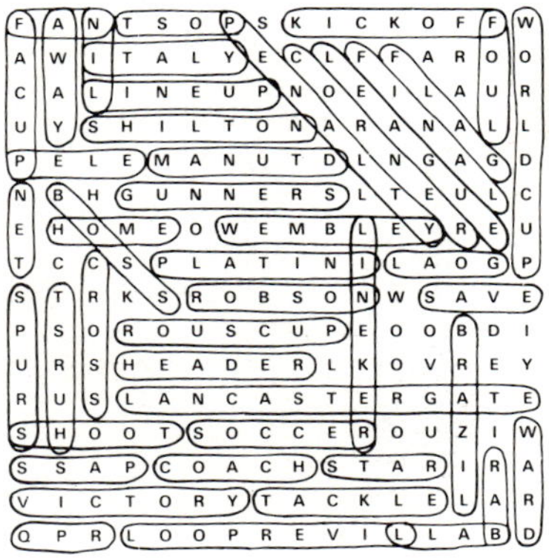

PICK